# THE BOY WITH TWO HEARTS

# THE BOY WITH TWO HEARTS

## A Story of Hope

### HAMED AMIRI

ICON

Published in the UK and USA in 2020
by Icon Books Ltd, Omnibus Business Centre,
39–41 North Road, London N7 9DP
email: info@iconbooks.com
www.iconbooks.com

Sold in the UK, Europe and Asia
by Faber & Faber Ltd, Bloomsbury House,
74–77 Great Russell Street,
London WC1B 3DA or their agents

Distributed in the UK, Europe and Asia
by Grantham Book Services, Trent Road,
Grantham NG31 7XQ

Distributed in the USA
by Publishers Group West,
1700 Fourth Street, Berkeley, CA 94710

Distributed in Canada by Publishers Group Canada,
76 Stafford Street, Unit 300,
Toronto, Ontario M6J 2S1

Distributed in Australia and New Zealand
by Allen & Unwin Pty Ltd, PO Box 8500,
83 Alexander Street, Crows Nest, NSW 2065

Distributed in South Africa
by Jonathan Ball, Office B4, The District,
41 Sir Lowry Road, Woodstock 7925

Distributed in India by Penguin Books India,
7th Floor, Infinity Tower – C, DLF Cyber City,
Gurgaon 122002, Haryana

ISBN: 978-178578-619-8

Typeset in Bell MT by Marie Doherty

Printed and bound in Great Britain by
Clays Ltd, Elcograf S.p.A.

# CONTENTS

*To my older brother Hussein who was my role model, inspiration and my best friend for life; to my mother who has sacrificed so much for me to be alive, well and to have a normal life; to my dad who quietly put his life on the line for all of us and has been a soundboard for every problem I've ever had; to my younger brother who has always stood by my side no matter how bad it got.*

# CHAPTER 1

# Herat, home. 2000

There was nothing special about our house in Herat, but it was all I knew as home until I was ten years old. It was built of clay, like all the other houses in our neighbourhood, and it was made up of four fairly bare rooms, with Persian rugs covering the floors. We lived with the families of two of my Dad's brothers, so it was always full and busy, and my brothers and cousins and I were always causing trouble.

There was a kitchen area where Mum would make *kichiri*, and a sitting and dining room with no sofas or dining chairs, only patterned pillows or *nalincheh*. We didn't eat our meals at a table, but around the *sofra*, an eating area on the floor.

The Taliban had taken control of Herat before I could remember, and rules in the city were strict. Curfew was 8pm. No one went out after dark, and women weren't allowed to go anywhere on their own. Even us children had to be careful who we spoke to, what we said and how we said it. The Taliban were everywhere, so it wasn't a good idea to do anything to stand out.

I was the middle of three boys, the jokey troublemaker sandwiched between my cheeky, liked-by-all older brother Hussein and my quieter, more reserved little brother Hessam, and we were sheltered from most of what went on with the Taliban. But I would sometimes overhear the elders talking about what they did – stories of mercenaries decapitating civilians and quickly sealing the neck with hot wax so they could bet on which headless body would stay standing the longest.

Then, one bright, and surprisingly warm winter's day when I was ten, everything changed. I had run home to fetch our football – a crumpled piece of lightweight PVC wrapped in another torn plastic bag – and as I went into the house I could hear Mum's voice from the kitchen. She was practising a speech she was writing. Word that this speech was happening had spread around the community, but in hushed voices.

'We have the same rights as men!' She paused, repeated herself quietly, and then shouted it. 'We have the same rights as men!'

This kind of talk was normal in our house, but I knew it spelt danger. Mum's interest in women's rights had begun a few years ago when some of the other mothers in the neighbourhood had asked her to mentor their teenage daughters. Mum had a reputation for being an amazing cook, and she was brilliant at sewing. The neighbourhood mothers were keen for their daughters to learn the home skills they would need when they got married and, having only sons, Mum enjoyed teaching them. She treated them like daughters.

But as the girls she mentored came and went, Mum began to realise that once they got married they wouldn't be much more than servants for their new husbands. How could she prepare them for that? The Taliban rule meant that girls had few rights anyway – they weren't allowed to go to school and had no choice but to wear the full burka. Outside the home they were considered useless.

Mum was going to give her speech the next day, which was a Friday. The community would be coming together for *Jummah*, the Friday prayers, and as many people as possible would hear it. But that meant it wouldn't just be the women she was trying to help who would be listening; the Taliban would hear it too.

I watched from the living room as Mum moved around the kitchen, making the dinner and practising her speech. Then Dad came in.

Dad was Mum's biggest fan. He was always getting under her feet and bustling around the kitchen, but he always supported her. He didn't look like most Afghans – he was fair-skinned with hazel eyes – and he had run a china shop with one of his brothers before opening the pharmacy where he now worked. Family was everything to him, and he backed Mum's ambitions to fight for female equality. But he also loved us all and wanted to protect his family, and he knew Mum's speech was dangerous. Opposing the Taliban publicly would put all of us in danger, and over the last few days we'd noticed his nerves starting to show.

'Where are the boys?' he said now. 'The whole neighbourhood knows about your speech. I really hope you know what you're doing.'

Mum looked up from the stove for a second and then turned back to what she was doing.

'They're playing football,' she said. 'And don't worry about tomorrow – we have God on our side.'

I crept out and went to find my brothers.

Our football pitch was a dusty alley in the neighbourhood where we had piled rocks up as goalposts. It was quite late when I arrived back with the ball, and the sun was already going down. I was always on the same team as my brother Hussein and played behind him, moving around the pitch so he was always in my sight. Although Hussein was four years older than me, Mum had trained me to keep a watchful eye over him, and I was always looking for any sign that he was in trouble.

Hussein had had a rare heart condition since he was born. He'd already had two operations in India: one when he was just a baby and another when he was six. But he'd got worse as he got older, and despite trips to Iran and Bulgaria to get help we were told that the only place he could get proper treatment was the UK or America. We knew that one day Hussein's illness would catch up with him and we would have to leave Afghanistan, but for us that seemed far in the future.

In the meantime, I had become an expert at checking up on Hussein, watching his breathing, the way he moved and the colour of his skin. I took my responsibility very seriously.

Now, as I looked down the alley, I saw Hussein's eyes light up as he spotted a gap in the opposition's defence. He chased a perfectly placed through-ball. 'Go on, Roberto Carlos!' I shouted.

But as he powered off the line and skipped past his marker, he suddenly stopped and hunched over. I panicked. I could hear Mum's voice in my head repeating her instructions: 'Take his pulse, then get help.'

There was a beat of silence, then I took a breath and ran towards him.

'Bro! You okay?' I said, trying to sound calm. By the time I reached him he had crouched down in the dust, his skinny shoulders rounded. He looked up at me, panting.

'Yeah, I'm fine.'

We'd been running around, he had raced down the pitch to get the ball, maybe he was just thirsty? No. I had a bad feeling about this.

I put my fingers on the right side of Hussein's neck just as Mum had shown me and began counting. 'One, two … wait …!' I couldn't keep up. It felt like machine-gun fire. My mind went blank for a moment, then I picked him up and put his right arm over my shoulder. I had seen football players carrying off their injured teammates like this. I could be a hero.

As we began stumbling home, I kept my fingers on Hussein's wrist and eventually his pulse dropped to match mine. Of course, then he was quick to tell me that he could carry himself, so I let go but kept an arm around his shoulder.

As we turned the corner to our street, we could hear something loud and rumbling. Jeeps. These ancient Russian military vehicles were a common sight in our neighbourhood, and the militia in them would yell at each other and taunt passers-by. It was all just intimidation, and it became a bit of a game to us. We would duck out of sight and pretend we were in a war film.

This time, Hussein and I rolled under an old Volga. We began counting the passing vehicles. There were too many – way more than normal. This wasn't just intimidation; they must be after something.

'Mum!' whispered Hussein.

As the jeeps got further away, we decided to follow, picking up the pace. I knew Mum was at home with Hessam, our little brother, and now Dad was there too, and the militia were heading in their direction.

But I also didn't want Hussein to start clutching his chest again. I prayed for the best and ran as fast as I could, Hussein following just behind me. As I hopped over the mud walls, I counted each footstep against Hussein's to make sure he was keeping up.

'Go on without me,' he said. But Mum had made me swear to never leave his side. She'd kill me if I left him here. At each junction I stopped, peering round the corner to check for danger and to allow Hussein to catch up. As the clay house came into view, we saw the convoy making its way down our street. My heart thumped. We ducked into the crumbling house opposite us and watched in silence, our panting gradually slowing as we caught our breath. The jeeps weren't stopping.

They rumbled further down the road and we sat back, relieved. But I was so angry. How dare they intimidate us like that? I picked up a broken brick and started to run after the jeeps. But Hussein grabbed me and put his arms around me from behind.

'Don't! Are you mad?' he said. His heart was racing against my back and I knew I had to calm him down. I dropped the brick and kicked it.

'Sorry, bro.'

*

That night we were all quiet around the *sofra*. Hessam and I sat either side of Hussein as usual, but instead of squabbling and joking we all quietly fidgeted on the rug. The food was delicious as always, but it was difficult to enjoy it as all I could think about was what might happen when Mum gave her speech tomorrow. Finally, Dad broke the silence.

'Can't you tone down the speech, Fariba? Be less critical of the Taliban?' Although Dad was proud of what Mum was doing, I could tell he was nervous about what might happen.

Mum was quick to defend her cause. 'Like they tone down their injustice? Have you forgotten how they threw boiling water at my own mother?' She looked at him defiantly, and we were all silent again.

'What about the children? At least think about them,' Dad said.

Mum was growing impatient. 'Think about the children? Okay. Do you want your children to grow up in an Afghanistan run by thugs? This isn't about us *or* our children, Mohammed. We need to take back what they have taken from us. We need to take back our future.'

Dad looked at us and then back to Mum. 'You know I'm with you to the end, don't you, Fariba? Come what may? There's no going back now, that's all. God help us.'

As we carried on eating I looked across at Hussein. His lips were turning purple again. I quickly nudged Hessam, who made a gesture at Dad without Mum noticing. But when I looked back at Hussein I saw his colour returning.

Every night, Mum would tell us a story after tucking us in to bed. The three of us slept in the same small bedroom with its single barred window looking over the street. Mum would usually decide the story for us, but that night Hessam beat her to it.

'Mum, why did the Taliban throw hot water at grandmother? Does it give people fiery tempers like you?'

Mum settled herself at the foot of the bed, smiling.

'I'll tell you about your grandmother,' she said. 'There was a time in our city when there were schools just for girls, so they could get an education just like you. But the Taliban shut them down. Your grandmother – and others like her who fought for equal education – were violently humiliated …'

Grandma sounded like a fierce woman. I could see where Mum got it from. I wondered what I would fight for when I grew up.

CHAPTER 2

# The speech

The next day was Friday. As the three of us walked to school, neighbours, shopkeepers and acquaintances were quick to express their excitement for Mum's big day. We thanked each one nervously. 'We're so going to be taken hostage,' I said to Hussein, and he punched me.

Every street corner of our fifteen-minute walk felt like the end of the line. At school, the teacher wrote something on the blackboard about pomegranate seeds being like tiny rubies, but I couldn't concentrate. I was more focused on what the other boys were whispering. Even the class bullies were quieter today. Maybe they thought we were going to be taken hostage too.

Mum had told us to go straight to another school in the neighbourhood when the last bell rang. She would be giving her speech in the playground. As we walked through Herat there were women in the streets, lots of them, all heading the same way as us. There was a weird kind of energy, and I couldn't work out if this was good or bad. My imagination ran wild. Perhaps Taliban informers had betrayed Mum's cause and were plotting another massacre?

As we arrived at the school, we saw a makeshift podium that clearly was able to be dismantled as quickly as it was put up. The audience, almost all of them women, were still arriving and there was hardly any room left in the playground. I thought I was good at counting, but I started running out of hundreds as I scanned the crowd. Apparently we were guests of honour, and we were ushered to the front to watch as Mum got ready to climb the wooden step ladder to the podium. Suddenly she came over and crouched down beside us. Her hands were shaking.

'You know I love you all,' she said. Her voice was trembling too. I couldn't work out whether she was scared or excited, but she kissed us all on the forehead and told us again how much she loved us. What was this? Was she saying goodbye?

Mum opened her speech with the usual 'God is great', and everyone went quiet. The people in the audience seemed as nervous as she was. I looked up at Mum and then at the crowd. People were nodding and shouting '*Inshallah!*' ('God willing!') as she spoke about making family values part of our vision of a new Afghanistan. I'd heard other people talking about this, so it was nothing unusual. But for a woman to stand up and talk about it like this in public was unheard of – and dangerous.

The rest of the speech was a blur. I remember a few bits – the Taliban, unity, extremism, freedom – and I remember the audience clapping and cheering. When Mum had nearly finished, she had to wait for the chants of 'Down with the Taliban' to stop before she could make herself heard. She finally ended by calling for unity and courage, and everyone clapped loudly.

Mum looked like a winner in a fight as she walked off the stage. We couldn't help but smile as she came towards us, and I felt so proud of her. Despite the laws on hugging and kissing in public, Dad gave her one of his signature bear hugs, and we giggled as the school headmaster ran over quickly to pull him away. Didn't Dad know that the rooftops of the houses all around had a view of the playground?

Mum kissed us again and I felt a sense of relief. But it didn't last long. Well-meaning supporters in the crowd were starting to surround Mum, jostling and pushing to get nearer. She tightened her grip on my hand. My other hand was holding Hussein's and I tightened my hold on him, trying not to fall over under all the people. I could hear voices asking Mum when they could visit her secretly. I could hardly stand up and the noise was terrifying.

'We must be cautious and smart …', I could hear her saying above the racket.

Then, as if by magic, the crowd disappeared. All those people were ready enough to rise to the challenge and make a difference, but they didn't want to be seen by the Taliban. It was fair enough. The Taliban were good at making examples of their enemies.

As we walked home Mum had never held our hands so tightly. We were proud of her, and I think she was proud of herself, but she seemed nervous. Everyone in the street was looking at us, nodding at Mum in support. Mum's speech wasn't just about her of course, but we still felt proud of what she'd done. She'd been watching the cruelty of the Taliban for years, and now she'd finally been able to stand up to them.

Although it felt good to see how proud the neighbourhood was of Mum, we couldn't wait to get home. We walked through the narrow streets and alleyways, Dad hurrying us along like a shepherd. He kept fussing at how slowly we were walking, and rushed us impatiently. He only seemed to relax when we could see our front door.

He half pushed us into the house and, looking around, locked the door behind us. This was a first – our door was hardly ever locked. So many of us lived in our house that there were always aunties and uncles, cousins and neighbours making their way in and out. Even though Herat was ruled by the Taliban, ours was a relatively safe neighbourhood on a quiet road, and there didn't feel much need for locked doors.

But I could feel Dad's relief. He bustled around Mum, trying to distract her and keep us all busy.

'Let's have a celebration!' he said. 'Our favourite meal to mark the occasion. It's been a great day, a memory we'll never forget. A lesson of faith and belief.'

This was all for our benefit of course – Dad wanting to show us it would all be okay. They didn't want to worry Hussein. But we weren't going to say no to our favourite dinner. While Mum prepared the meal, Dad kept his mind busy by watering the plants. He seemed on edge, but no matter how hard he tried, he couldn't hide the smile on his face.

We were a bit in awe of Mum that day. We'd never seen anyone stand up to the Taliban, let alone a woman. Mum's bravery was normal in our house, but this was the first time it had crossed into the outside world. We were proud. We couldn't stop talking about it, each going over our favourite part of the speech. For Hussein, it was seeing the faces of the women in the audience as they listened to Mum. For Hessam (mummy's boy), it was when Mum kissed him and made him feel like a VIP.

I said it was the moment at the end of the speech where, just for a second, I caught Mum's eye. I could see how happy she was, and I knew that she'd done something she really believed in. Mum wanted the little spark she'd created that day to grow into a big fire, and I wished she'd been able to do that.

There were no aunts, uncles or cousins for dinner tonight, just the five of us. This was a good thing: there would be more food for us. Mum had made our favourite lamb dish, *ghormeh plough,* and she batted my hand away as I tried to sneak some off the serving dish. It was gloomy outside, but inside our little sitting room was colourful and bright as slowly but surely the *sofra* was set and plate after plate of colourful food filled the floor. Meals like this were my favourite.

We sat down one by one, with Mum and Dad on each side to complete the circle. The circle was more than just a shape, Mum explained, which was why we all had to wait our turn to sit. 'Family is the most important thing,' she said. 'We don't know what lies ahead, but what we do know is that family, love and sticking together – no matter how tough or scary life is – that's the key.'

We were used to these life lessons of Mum's. But secretly we loved it. I started to understand why Mum had given her speech, despite all the danger. Food was forgotten for a minute, as we looked at each other silently. It was a strange moment that has stayed with me since that day – it was as if we were inside a bubble, oblivious to everything outside of our circle.

Just like any bubble, sooner or later it had to burst. As we ate together, we had no idea how life-changing the events of that day would be.

We weren't expecting anyone, but when the knock at the door came we still thought it must be one of our uncles. Dad walked cautiously towards the door. We all hoped for a friendly face as he asked loudly, 'Who is it?'

'It's me. Open the door, quick,' came a whisper. Relieved to hear the friendly voice of our uncle, or *amu*, Dad rushed to unlock the doors to embrace him. But we could tell something was up – his voice was panicked, and before Dad could even hug him or say hello he pushed the door shut behind him.

'Close the door, lock it!' he said. We'd never seen Uncle like this before. Dad looked worried.

'What is it? Is the family okay? Sister is unwell ... how is her health?'

Uncle looked past Dad at us sitting at the *sofra*. We rushed up to hug him, but his smile was fake. Even without Dad's worried face in the background, we knew something was wrong. Uncle's hug was tighter and lasted longer than usual. Reluctantly we went into our bedroom to let the adults talk.

Hessam was being annoying, and Hussein tried to distract him while I tried to listen in to the adults' conversation.

Uncle called Mum over, and we heard Dad say, 'Please, tell me what has happened. Is everyone okay?'

'They heard the speech,' he whispered. 'They're looking for you.'

'Okay,' said Dad. 'What else? Please, just tell us.'

Uncle spoke so quietly I could hardly make out what he said, but I heard, 'The *mullah* has given an order.'

This was it. All our fears in one sentence. We called the *mullah* the 'executioner', and we were terrified of him. He had turned our local football pitch into a place of execution, and it was now referred to as 'the pit'. People would gather there to hear death sentences passed on people who spoke up against the Taliban. Later they'd be executed. Someone must have told them about Mum, and now they wanted her dead.

CHAPTER 3

# The Amiri market

Although I'd always lived under Taliban rule, I never thought it would affect us like this. It had just been everyday life. We'd always known that Hussein's health meant we would one day have to seek help from doctors outside of Afghanistan, but we hadn't prepared for the fact that Afghanistan would no longer be a safe place for us. Despite all the troubles with the Taliban, Afghanistan was our home, a familiar place. I'd never known anything else. I realise now that home isn't where you live, it's the people you live with. And you can take them with you anywhere.

Now we were in danger, and the only thing to do was escape. I was a naturally nosy child, always listening at doorways, wanting to know what the adults were talking about. But this time my nosiness had led to me hearing something I didn't want to hear. I wanted to tell my brothers, but I knew the stress it would put on Hussein's heart, so I kept it to myself for now. I supposed they'd know soon enough.

Playing dumb, I moved away from the door and went back to Hessam and Hussein. Hessam didn't notice anything different, but I could tell Hussein could see that I knew something. He probably knew I was hiding it from him because of his illness too.

While we waited in the bedroom, the adults were debating in loud whispers in the other room. What were they talking about? How we could hide from the Taliban? Or how to find a way to get out? That would need money, which I knew we didn't have. It would also mean knowing the right people – the ones who went under false names, the ones who promised a safe haven. I already knew so many stories of people who had died trying to leave. Would it even be safe? Whatever my parents were discussing, I knew it would involve a journey, and I was terrified of it.

Finally, we could tell by the hugging and kissing that Uncle was leaving, and shortly afterwards we heard the front door being locked. It was time to face the music. Hussein wanted to go straight through to the other room, but I didn't want to, and tried to distract myself with toys. Eventually, Mum and Dad came through to us.

Dad was struggling for words, so Mum started.

'Firstly, I want you all to know that we'll be okay,' she said. 'As long as we're together.' We didn't say anything. 'Because of my speech, the *mullah* has made a decision. We're not safe here any more. We're going to need to leave quickly, and we're going to have to sell our things to raise enough money. There are people who can help us, but we have to

pay them before they'll do anything. Even if we sell everything we might not have enough. Then we're going to have
to go on a long journey, to a place we don't even know yet.
We didn't want this, but we've got no choice. And we *will*
be okay.'

When Mum had finished, Dad asked if we had any questions. For some reason, at that point we didn't have much
to ask, although afterwards I thought of a hundred things I
wanted to know. Uncle was going to try to buy us some time,
but our only chance of survival lay in the hands of traffickers.
They only spoke one language: money, so the first thing to
do was to raise as much as we could.

In a community like ours, fear of the Taliban brought
people together, but we were soon to learn the strength of
the love and respect for our family in our neighbourhood. The
next day friends and family gathered in secret, and within
a few hours of the word spreading our house had become a
market. Everything we had – from dishes and cooking uten-
sils to toys and books – was for sale. There was no time to
price things up, we just needed enough money to pay for our
escape. Mum laid everything out like a bazaar: clothes, rugs,
curtains and bedspreads were draped across furniture, while
bowls and crockery were stacked in corners. Our neighbours
poured into the house, picking up items and offering money.
It was unlike any market we'd ever seen. No one haggled, and
people even paid over the odds for items they didn't want or
need. We couldn't believe the support from our community.

The Amiri market was fun, and Hessam and I enjoyed
showing people our belongings and counting the money.
Mum was quiet though, and I realised that this must be hard

for her. She was selling everything she owned, the memories and the laughter from our house, in a scuffle of people she knew well. Hessam insisted on selling his favourite toy, saying he'd grown out of it anyway, but this seemed to upset Mum more.

Within a few hours the Amiri market was closed, leaving us with four bare walls and the clothes we stood up in.

'I'm sorry, boys,' Mum kept saying. But we didn't think of it like that. Why should she be sorry? Yes, she was the one who had given the speech, but we all believed in what she was doing. We were a family, and families stick together, remember?

So our house was empty but our hearts were full. Our friends and neighbours had helped us when we really needed it, and we felt like a team standing up to the Taliban. I hoped that Mum's speech was just the beginning, that somehow what she'd started would carry on after we'd left. I also hoped that we'd be able to come home one day.

Raising the money to pay the traffickers was only half the problem. Our real enemy was time. Dad's next mission was to find the right people who could help with our escape, and so began a frantic search for someone who could put us in touch with a contact. We never asked where we were heading – it didn't seem to matter. Our destination wasn't important, as long as it wasn't Herat.

While Dad was busy trying to connect with the underground trafficking world, Mum helped us to pack. After the market we didn't have much – just two sets of clothes each. But we didn't really miss our toys and books. We knew that life was about surviving now.

As we packed we teased and jostled with each other as brothers do, but Mum was deep in thought. 'Are you okay, Mum?' Hussein asked.

'Yes,' she said, 'I'm just thinking about all the women we're leaving behind. The women I've been fighting for.'

She looked disappointed, but I knew it wasn't just that. As she stared at the empty rooms I knew that she was heart-broken to leave the house where she'd married, where she'd brought us up and created all our memories. I realised that we were leaving our friends and family too. Would we ever see our cousins again?

As it started to get dark, the only fruits of Dad's enquiries were that we would hear back soon. But would 'soon' be soon enough? We knew that the Taliban were out there searching for Mum. Were they scouring the streets for her? Could they find her right here, in our house? No one ate much that evening, and the *sofra* was a different place to the night before.

CHAPTER 4

# Escape on the roof

That night, after the market, we rolled our clothes under our heads as pillows and talked each other to sleep. Our spare jumpers became duvets for the night and the house felt empty and cold. I slept okay, but I woke to the sound of loud hammering on the door.

I sat up in bed and saw that Hussein was already up, and panicking. I tried to keep him calm: now would not be a good time for him to have an episode. I talked to him calmly as he stood shivering in the bedroom, and I could tell that he was trying to calm himself down.

'Go, take the boys,' I heard Dad whisper to Mum, his eyes on the door. This was no time to argue. Mum came running in and grabbed us, and we ran up to the roof. It was freezing up there, but we sat, waiting, behind the clay chimney. I could feel Hussein's hand in mine, sweaty, shaking. 'Please

God, look after his heart, look after his heart, look after his heart,' I kept repeating in my head.

We heard some noises downstairs, and Dad's voice questioning the visitors. Then we heard something terrible. A bang. We looked at each other in horror. Mum put her hand over her mouth, but we knew we had to stay silent. I couldn't bear it. I could feel the panic rising up in my chest. Then there was chaos in the garden downstairs, and we couldn't hear Dad at all among all the shouting and heavy footsteps. For a minute I was terrified that they were coming up to the roof and would find us there. Would they kill us? Had they killed Dad?

We could hear the Taliban coming into the house and making their way through all the rooms. There was nothing to take, nothing left at all. But what if they were looking for us? Mum seemed in a trance, and we tugged on her to snap her out of it. Then we heard a quiet hissing noise from across the neighbour's roof.

'Psst, psst.' What was it? Suddenly we realised that a ladder was being placed across the two rooftops.

'Over here,' came a voice. It was Uncle! I grabbed the ladder and pulled it across the gap between the houses. We had to be quick – the Taliban weren't going to stop looking for Mum. She wasn't moving, so I grabbed her by the wrist and Hussein and I dragged her across the roof onto the ladder. One by one we scrambled across to the neighbour's roof and hugged Uncle. Even in the chaos I remember he smelt like Dad, and I tried not to think about what might have happened.

Mum was silent for the rest of the day. She seemed to have lost all emotion. Uncle put on a brave face and organised everything, taking us to a neighbour's house until we were sure the Taliban had gone. Then he left, I didn't know where to. Was it to find Dad? Or to carry on where he left off, trying to find someone who could get us out of Afghanistan? But how could we leave without Dad? That was impossible.

That evening was gloomy, and for the first time Mum seemed really angry. Dad had stood by her through every-thing – it wasn't fair that we didn't know what had happened to him. At dinner with our neighbours the circle felt empty, incomplete.

I was worried about Hussein, too. Mum had always been there to look after his health, but now she seemed distant, preoccupied. Did that mean I was in charge? I kept replaying what had happened on the roof in my mind. Mum said she'd heard a shot, but I wasn't so sure.

Just before bedtime that night, Uncle came back. We were desperate for news of Dad, but were afraid of what he might say. He'd been crying and was out of breath. Surely that was a bad sign?

'It's your Dad – he's alive,' he said. We ran towards him and squeezed him.

'How?' we demanded. Uncle rubbed his face and began to explain how the Taliban had taken Dad and were holding him captive. As far as he knew he was okay, but we had to get him out as soon as we could. He'd also managed to find some traffickers who could help us get out of the country.

Mum came in and rushed to us. She was crying. 'What can we do?' she said. 'How can we find him?'

'We know where he is,' said Uncle. 'It's just a case of getting to him. But I've got a plan. I'm going to go with the cousins tonight and try to get him out.'

'They'll have your throats,' said Mum, nervously.

'We'll be okay,' he replied. 'Anyway, we have no choice. The Taliban aren't patient, and the traffickers are ready to take you as soon as the whole family is ready.'

'Take us? Now?' Mum hesitated. We were leaving. As soon as we got Dad back we'd be leaving Afghanistan forever.

It wasn't until afterwards that I discovered what happened that night when they rescued Dad. Uncle had used his connections through the pharmacy to find out where Dad was and paid off the security guard to persuade him to look the other way. Dad was in a pretty bad state when they found him, and it was a struggle to get him home in one piece. They'd more or less had to carry him through the streets, the cousins walking ahead to make sure it was clear.

That was the last time Dad saw his cousins.

We waited impatiently at our neighbour's house, looking for any sign of Uncle and the rescue party. The trafficker was already outside, his foot on the pedal, the engine running. He said it was important to make the most of the cover of darkness, to get as many miles behind us as possible before daybreak.

I remember how annoying the engine noise was, and how the car lights shone down the street as we peered from the window into the darkness. I kept watching that space, waiting for any sign of Dad and the cousins. Finally, in the distance I could see a group of men walking up the lit-up street. It was them! Behind the cousins I could see Dad, walking slowly and with a limp. Uncle's arm was around his shoulder, holding him up. He looked battered, bruised, but he was alive.

So those were our last moments in Afghanistan. It wasn't a great goodbye – in the dimly lit street with the fumes of a car engine – but it was the last time we would see our house, our uncles and aunts, our cousins, our neighbours. Then everything changed.

# CHAPTER 5

# Moscow

We were told to get into the boot of the car, and the driver showed us a small hidden compartment underneath a fake top, so that if someone were to open the boot it would look like it was empty. There wasn't much room, but we all bundled into it and tried to get comfortable. I could hear Dad's rasping breathing, and we knew he must have broken ribs.

In any other circumstances we would have been excited about our first trip away from Herat. But this wasn't what we'd imagined. We couldn't see anything, and even the driver was obscured by a screen so that border guards wouldn't be able to see into the back.

All we could do was hope that this journey would lead to a better life. I couldn't even dream of what that would be like, but I wanted it to be somewhere where we could finally let our guard down and not worry about life and death. Somewhere we would be safe and could grow up to have a normal life. Somewhere Hussein could get better. Somewhere with no AK47s.

All of that felt so far off right now as we lay in the cramped space, knowing there would be a long journey ahead of us.

We were unable to keep track of time, but after what must have been days we came to a stop. Outside the car we could hear a commotion, and the driver told us not to make a noise. I wanted to follow instructions to the letter, so I held my breath. Not breathing in through my nose was actually a relief, as the smell in the car had become pretty bad. Hussein and Hessam copied me, and there was complete silence in the compartment.

Outside the car we could hear bad language and men talking aggressively. They were swearing at each other, but then they laughed. Finally we were taken out, put into another van, and we started moving again.

Here we were allowed to sit in the back, and as I looked out of the car window I could see the sky was pitch black. It was freezing – the coldest it had been since we left home – and the road was much bumpier than before. After a while I could see lights, and there were buildings – taller than I'd ever seen before, and I wondered if we were in a city.

Soon after that we stopped and again were all told to get out. The only thing I remember is that every bit of my body, from my neck to my legs, clicked as I unfolded myself from the car. I actually quite enjoyed this, as I always loved clicking my knuckles to make my brothers groan.

We stepped out of the car into huge dirty piles of snow at the side of the road. That explained why we'd been so cold in the car for the last few hundred miles. Dad pointed towards a metal door by an entrance to an apartment and followed us to let us in.

'Moscow.' Dad said. 'We're almost there.' I didn't know what this meant. Almost where? We didn't even know where we were going. He smiled brightly, but I could sense he was uneasy.

The apartment was pretty dreadful, but it was a roof over our heads after days and nights of being in the back of cars and vans, so we were just happy to be out of that cramped space.

That night we all had the best sleep we had had for a while. It felt so good to rest on an actual bed instead of being cramped in a tiny compartment in a moving van. I couldn't help but imagine what lay ahead – we'd been dreaming of getting somewhere safe for every hour, minute we were on the road that I started to wonder whether such a place actually existed. And even if it did, would we ever get there? Would we ever be safe?

The next morning, as the sunlight came through the blinds I tried to fight against waking up. We were all desperate for more sleep, but soon I could hear Mum pottering about in the little kitchen. Before long familiar smells reached my nostrils.

I kicked my brothers awake, and we dragged ourselves to the rusty dining table to eat our first proper breakfast in what felt like ages. It was only tea, bread and cheese, but it was so good. We devoured everything, fighting over the last crumbs of bread as usual, and then bickered over who would help clear up.

There was a TV in the apartment, but when I turned it on all the channels were in Russian. We didn't care too much, as having a working TV felt like luxury, even if it was in a different language. We found a show we liked about a man who talked to his car – it was sleek and black with red lights and we'd never seen anything like it. We were glued to it.

Dad decided to go for a walk, which was odd, because he only did this when he wanted to clear his head. I took my eyes off the TV for a second to watch after him and wondered what he was worrying about. Was it just the future, or had something happened that we didn't know about? I hated being kept in the dark, and I was always worrying that Mum and Dad were hiding bad news from us. I always assumed the worst. Was Hussein getting worse? Were we being followed? It was Dad's job to keep us safe, and he always had until now, but what about things that were out of his control? How could he keep us safe when he had no idea what was coming next?

The weather was freezing, and walking the snowy streets wasn't my idea of fun, so we spent our time watching bad Russian TV, fighting and moping about. I don't know how many days we were in the apartment, but since we'd got there Dad was the only one of us who'd been outside. Eventually, boredom got the better of us, and we decided to venture out.

Dad suggested that we go to the local market to buy essentials such as bread, cheese and milk. So we each put our two pairs of trousers on, together with all the sweaters we could find. We even wore two pairs of socks.

I'd noticed how the Russians seemed to love doors. At home we only had one door, and apart from during those final few days, it was more or less always open. Here, as soon as you walked out of one door there was immediately another one! A wooden door behind a metal door. These Russians certainly seemed to take their security seriously.

There was a cold wind when we stepped outside and it picked the snow dust off the ground and swirled it around. We'd never walked on a thick sheet of impacted snow before. The streets were so quiet they were spooky, and the city felt dangerous, even after our experience of living in Herat.

Mum told me not to be so silly, but Dad held our hands tightly as we walked through the streets to the market, and I could see that Mum was also nervous. I knew when we were getting close to the market, as I could smell all sorts of exotic foods being cooked.

'*Idi syuda, idi syuda*' ('Come here') was all I could hear from the shopkeepers. They were terrifying – much larger than the men we were used to in Afghanistan – and they looked so aggressive with all their shouting and gesturing.

But Hussein and Hessam and I were easily distracted by the colours and noise of the market, and before long we were running in and out of the stalls. Suddenly a gentle voice came behind us, '*Ty khochesh' sladkogo?*' ('You want a sweet?') and a tall man stood behind us, with three sweets held out in his palm. I didn't hesitate, and grabbed the lollipop he was holding, unwrapping it and putting it straight in my mouth. Dad came rushing over, embarrassed, and offered money to the man in broken Russian, but he refused to take anything and just smiled at us.

We continued to wander through the market, in and out of the maze of busy stalls enjoying our sweets. Suddenly we realised we'd walked into quite a different area of the market. The atmosphere had changed – it wasn't as warm as before, and I could feel people staring down at us. Was it the way we looked? Could they hear that we weren't speaking in Russian? I started to realise that the people were mostly staring at Mum, at the scarf she used to cover her hair. I spat out the lollipop and put my hand in hers. But they kept on staring.

It was like a standoff. We stood there holding hands, and they stood there staring. Suddenly someone brushed past Mum's handbag, and she shifted it across her body. She'd been holding on to it tightly the whole time we were at the market, as we knew there would be thieves about.

But then she checked her bag, opening it to feel inside. Her hand went straight out the other side. There was a perfectly clean cut on the outside of the bag, made by some sort of blade. The bag was empty.

We had been tricked. We quickly realised that the sweets had been a decoy – a distraction while the thief was at work. It wasn't just the contents of a handbag, it was everything, all the money we had in the world. For a long time afterwards I would trust no one, and was always suspicious of someone doing a kind act.

Mum was patient as usual, but Dad was livid. It was his idea to leave the apartment and he hadn't been able to protect us. We'd sold everything, left our family and friends, travelled hundreds of miles, and for what? Is this what our 'safe haven' looked like? How could someone do something like this?

Mum reminded him that for the people at the market, we were no different from any other foreigners. They didn't know the trauma we'd been through already, that we'd had to leave our home and family.

It was then that we realised how alone we were. We had no home, no belongings, no identity. We were nobodies: stateless and on the run. Mum had stood up for what she believed in – what we all believed in – and as a result we had to leave everything we knew. It was so unfair. It felt like we could be running forever, and that we'd never find a safe place to live. But Hussein needed somewhere he could get better, and every day of being on the road put an extra strain on his health. The longer we took, the longer it would be until he could get the treatment he needed.

So we left the market with less than we'd arrived with. We'd managed to buy some bread and some cheese before the money was stolen, and now we hadn't got a penny. All the money we'd saved, everything we'd raised from selling our belongings, was gone.

We got back to the apartment, huddled together in the living room and turned on the TV. Watching the man with his car with the red lights again, we ate the cheese and bread together and went to bed.

The next morning we had a small breakfast of more bread and cheese, with Mum and Dad going without so there was enough for us. Dad left the apartment soon after breakfast to make some calls back home to try and get some money from one of our uncles. We couldn't bear the idea of more bread and cheese.

Hours went by, but eventually Dad returned with a smile on his face.

'I managed to make some calls,' he said. 'And I've got us enough money to last us the next few weeks.'

The relief was immediate. We didn't know what would happen after that, but for now we were okay. We decided to celebrate by going on a trip, so once again we doubled up our clothes, looking around for anything else we could put on to avoid the cold.

All wrapped up, we left the apartment through the prison-like doors again and walked to the nearest bus stop.

Mum was anxious and kept reminding us that every stranger could be a thief. I imagined every passer-by to be a potential attacker too, inspired by the TV shows we'd been watching. I stayed glued to Mum and slightly behind the rest of the family. Hussein held Hessam's hand and stuck close to Dad.

After a few bus stops and a short walk, we found ourselves in a different part of town. Above and around us were golden buildings, taller and grander than anything we'd seen before. I still stuck close to Mum, but was distracted by the amazing scenery of the Kremlin and St Basil's Cathedral.

As we were enjoying the sights and the novelty of there being no snow on the pavements, I suddenly felt the sensation of being watched. Sure enough, across the street was a group of policemen staring at us, and after a minute or two they started to walk over. I froze. We had no documents, and if they asked us for proof of identity they'd deport us without a second thought. I knew I had to distract them, and after watching so much TV I knew exactly how to do it. I whispered to Mum, 'I'll see you at home. *Go*,' and suddenly darted out of the crowd. I headed straight for the two burly police officers, praying that Mum and Dad would take the others home like I told them.

Thankfully, Dad started to steer the others away, trying not to attract attention in the crowd. The police were looking only at me now, as I charged towards them like a mad thing. I didn't have a plan for when I reached them, so as soon as I got near I darted away again, changing my direction towards a small alleyway.

The adrenaline was rushing through my veins now, and my only aim was to get away and find my way back to the apartment. But how would I do that? I didn't know the language and couldn't even read the signs.

*Just keep running*, I thought. So I forced my legs to keep going, darting through alleyways and narrow streets until I was sure that I'd lost them. The only thing I could think of was to follow the bus route we had taken to get here, through the backstreets to the apartment. Perhaps the police would get tired or bored, or perhaps I'd be able to outrun them.

Then I could hear the police behind me, shouting in Russian, but I couldn't stop now – I just had to find a way to shake them off. Suddenly I realised I was somewhere familiar. The market! I hated this place, but it could just give me the cover I needed to get them off my tail.

I suddenly changed direction again, my legs like springs, and headed towards the market. I knew the little huts that covered the stalls would confuse them, and maybe they'd get distracted by all the thieves about, too.

I ran past the bread stall, the cheese man and the man giving out sweets. *I must be able to lose them in here.* I was pretty sure that I knew the way back home from here, but there was no way I was going to let them follow me there. So I kept running, darting in and out of the stalls, until I looped past the far side of the market and realised they'd lost sight of me for just a second. Being small, I was able to hide behind the large men on the market stalls, and finally I came to a stop behind some burly stall holders.

I could see them but they couldn't see me. They looked confused for a minute, then started to walk in the opposite direction.

After a few more minutes just to be on the safe side, I followed the route back to the apartment, looking over my shoulder every few steps to make sure no one was following. As I approached the apartment I could see Dad pacing around outside, his face pale, and Mum up in the window, anxiously looking out onto the street.

'Dad!' I called, running towards him. I'd been so brave – excited almost – when the police were chasing me, but now the tears came and I sobbed and sobbed.

'Don't ever do anything like that again,' Dad said firmly, but as I tried to talk through my sobs he interrupted me. 'I know, I know. Thank you.' I held on to him for sheer relief.

After we went back into the flat nothing much was said about my adventure. Mum put the TV on for us and we went back to normal – whatever 'normal' was. We didn't need to talk about how close it was, what could have happened if I'd been caught.

# CHAPTER 6

# Pomogite!

'Wake up, wake up!' I was half asleep but could hear Dad shouting at me. He was thrusting an ice hockey stick into my hand, but I was drowsy and had no clue why. Hussein was already up, although his eyes were half closed, and he was standing by my bed holding a baseball bat. Hessam was still fast asleep next to me.

We'd been in Moscow for several months now, waiting and waiting for the call to say someone could help us to move on. We'd built a life for ourselves and met some other refugee families who were also waiting to be moved on. We still hadn't got used to the cold though.

'What's going on?' I asked, shivering. My heart was racing by now, as I knew something was very wrong. I could hear a commotion outside, and my body ran cold as I realised there was someone out there, in the building, trying to get into the flat. Scenes from TV shows went through my mind and I was visualising what I would do if an intruder attacked me, when there was a bang from the metal door.

There was someone outside – maybe even a few people – and they were trying to unlock the door. We could hear the clicking and scratching of metal as they tried to force it open. Was it mafia? Were they trying to rob us?

'I'm going to call one of the other refugees,' Dad said, and he went to the phone. Not knowing anything else to do, we went to the windows and opened them, screaming '*Pomogite, pomogite!*' ('Help!') into the darkness outside. It was one of the few words we'd learnt since being here.

We kept screaming until our neighbours in the nearby apartments woke up, but instead of helping us they only shouted back, 'What do you want?'

'*Pomogite, pomogite!*' We continued to shout. We didn't know how to explain what was happening, so could only repeat this one word.

I could hear Dad on the phone, and he came off and told us that it would be okay, it was normal, and it would be 40 minutes before Dad's friend could come. Normal? How could this be normal? And what were we supposed to do until then? We couldn't call the police as we didn't have a valid visa or any documentation, so we'd have to defend the apartment on our own. If it was mafia then we were in trouble, as they didn't care who got hurt. We could be fighting for our lives.

I planned to aim for the knees – I'd seen that somewhere – and then I'd go for the head and try to get them to drop whatever they were carrying. In my mind I was a warrior, but the reality was that we were little boys with ice hockey sticks and baseball bats. We had no chance.

Dad kept motioning to us and trying to look through the peephole to see if he could get a glimpse of our attackers, but because of the double doors no light was coming through from the hallway. He said the men seemed to be kneeling down and trying to open the locks, and I could hear rattling and scratching.

Mum was with Hussein now, trying to keep him calm so his heart rate wouldn't increase. Heightened emotion had been known to cause another attack in the past. But how could we stay calm when there were people outside our door trying their very best to get in?

Through it all, unbelievably, Hessam was still asleep. We stood there for ten minutes, then twenty, then half an hour as we waited for something to happen. I could feel my eyes starting to close, but still we could hear rattling at the door. Still our attackers didn't materialise.

'They can't be very good robbers,' I said, and Dad glared at me. He went to the peephole and looked again to see if he could see anything in the pitch black. Suddenly there was a loud bang and he shot back from the door. Hussein shouted 'I'm ready!' and held his bat above his head, ready to charge.

Dad jumped in front of him, gripping his own bat, and Mum looked panicked. There was another loud bang. Dad looked through the peephole. There was nothing to see, no attackers, nothing. A mystery. I almost wished something would happen. I was like a coiled spring waiting to be released. Then the noise began again, a scratching and grinding on the rusty metal door.

'I can't see anything,' Dad said as he looked through the door again. 'I think I'm going crazy.'

Then the phone rang and we all jumped out of our skin. It was Dad's friend, saying he was nearly at the apartment. Dad spoke to him for a few minutes and explained what was happening, then he suddenly put his hand over the phone and shouted to us, 'Go and get the black pepper!'

I wasn't sure I'd heard him right, but I ran to the kitchen and grabbed the pepper.

'Pour it by the door,' Dad whispered, and I dumped the whole bag by the door and ran back, picking up my stick again.

Now Dad approached the door slowly, and we realised with horror that he was going to open it. I screwed up my eyes and prepared myself for the thugs standing behind it. Nothing happened.

Instead we were left looking at the hallway, and the remains of what looked like breadcrumbs on the floor. It was almost as if something had tried to *eat* its way through the door.

'He was right,' Dad said with relief. 'Rats.'

We jumped. 'Rats?' we said in disbelief. How could rats have caused all that noise?

'Is that what the pepper was for?' asked Mum.

'Yes,' said Dad. 'My friend said there are huge rats in this building and the only thing that deters them is the strong taste of pepper. You can drop your bats, boys.'

We put down our weapons. Rats? Huge rats? I had been ready for anything, ready to protect my family against murderous thugs. But as I walked back to bed I shivered. The thought of rats was worse.

\*

After six months in Moscow, we had begun to think of it as a sort of home. We had developed a routine as a family and I was enjoying the TV shows, especially *Knight Rider*. But we knew our journey must continue at some point, as Russia couldn't offer Hussein the medical treatment he so desperately needed. As the months went by I didn't notice him deteriorating, but Mum and Dad must have known he was getting weaker, as they seemed anxious to move on.

As for Hussein, he always seemed to take everything in his stride. His default setting was to put others before himself, and he was always more concerned that Hessam and I were okay. He was also protective over Mum and Dad, and he'd do anything to stop them worrying about him.

I had mixed feelings when Dad told us a contact had been in touch and we could move on. I didn't want to leave this apartment as it was all we'd known for a while, but on the other hand I was keen to get to a safer location. Either way, we had no choice – the call had come, we'd be leaving tonight.

It wasn't the first time we'd had to move at a moment's notice, so it didn't take us long to pack up our belongings. We were to wait until 11pm, when we would be picked up from the apartment by a trafficker, under cover of darkness.

Mum was calm as usual, but I'd grown to understand that this was mostly for our benefit. Over the past months we'd all become much more aware of what was going on, even Hessam, who continued to play the baby. In some ways we were no longer children, but partners with Mum and Dad in what we were trying to do. We'd had to grow up in the last few months, and I suppose I'd always been older than my years, as I had the constant responsibility of watching out for Hussein. And as for Hussein, he was used to facing challenges.

I remember feeling genuinely frightened that night as we waited to be collected. We didn't know what would happen to us, where we were going or whether it was safe. As always, we were entirely in the hands of the traffickers.

The clock ticked on and 11pm came and went. We were restless, but I struggled to keep my eyes open. I must have dropped off, because suddenly I was jolted awake by the phone ringing. Dad quickly answered, then put it down and said, 'We've got to be ready in 30 minutes.'

As always, we wrapped ourselves in several layers and mentally said goodbye to the 'home' we'd known for the last few months. It had kept us safe for the most part.

At around 2am the men came to collect us, and Dad locked the door to the apartment and handed them the keys. We were shown to a waiting car and bundled into the back once more. Dad was able to sit in the front as, with his unusual hazel eyes, he didn't look as 'foreign' as we did.

I was dreading another long journey, never knowing when you were going to stop to go to the toilet or when you would get any food. As we settled into the boot all we could see out of the tops of the windows was the dark sky and fewer and fewer buildings as we left the city.

Hessam fell asleep and I could see Mum praying silently under her breath. I couldn't see Dad's face in the front, but I could tell by how upright he was sitting that he was tense.

Minutes became hours, and we had few stops for toilet breaks. Each time we did get out of the car we were somewhere more remote, and there were hardly any people around. It must have been the early hours of the morning, but it was still dark outside.

Suddenly the car took a sharp right onto a bumpy road and we were thrown around in the boot with no warning. Hessam started from his sleep and the lights of the car were turned off. We were told to stay quiet, and once again I found myself holding my breath so I wouldn't make a sound.

We came to an abrupt stop and the engine was turned off. Translating in my head, I could just work out someone saying to Dad, 'Get out and take your kids.'

We uncurled ourselves from the boot, glad to stretch our legs, but not having a clue where we were. The gloomy early morning light hit our eyes and we blinked, squinting into the pale sky.

'Where are we?' asked Hessam, as in front of us was an opening into what I can only describe as a jungle. It was like a scene from a movie: there were huge leaves and thick undergrowth and the trees were so tall they blocked out a lot of the light. Some of the leaves were bigger than Dad.

'Wait here,' said the driver, and he hurried back to his car.

I could see the panic on Dad's face. Where was he going? He couldn't just leave us here in the jungle! What were we supposed to do? Before we could shout after him, our driver started the engine and drove off. And there we were, left in the eerie quiet of the early morning, in the middle of nowhere, with no idea of where we were or what to do.

'It'll be fine,' said Dad unconvincingly. 'He'll be back, it's fine.' But in truth we had no idea whether he'd be back. What was to stop him from taking our money and then leaving us in the middle of nowhere?

We found a low branch and settled down to wait. It was good to stretch out our legs, but we were cold and hoped we wouldn't have to wait for too long. Dad stood nearby, watching for the returning car, while Mum took out some dry bread from a bag, handing us each a piece.

I started to grow more and more impatient as the hours went by. Then, just as we started to believe we really had been left to find our own way, Dad whispered, 'Shhhhh, I can hear something.' He turned, cautiously, to the clearing where the car had dropped us, and sure enough we could see a four-by-four approaching from around the corner.

Dad's guard was up. 'This must be them,' he said firmly.

The four-by-four pulled up and a man got out. 'Get in,' he ordered, and without hesitation we jumped into the car.

I wonder now in what other circumstances you would get into the car of a complete stranger in the middle of a jungle. And yet we were so relieved to see someone, to not be abandoned in the middle of nowhere, that we would have done anything without question. We were desperate, and it had become normal for us to do what strangers told us.

'Hold tight,' said the driver, and he wasn't joking. He started the engine and charged towards the thick jungle ahead, the four-by-four breaking down undergrowth as we went. There wasn't a clear path ahead, so we just made one ourselves, the branches scratching and scraping against the paintwork.

It felt like he was testing our limits, trying to scare us. The jungle seemed to be getting even denser, and he didn't slow down when we hit bumps – in fact, he seemed to speed up. We were being thrown around inside the vehicle like rag dolls and my head hit the ceiling several times.

Eventually, the car slowed down and we saw that we were approaching a clearing. In it was a group of people surrounded by what we assumed were more traffickers. Dad called them 'mercenaries', which I suppose is what they were, as they were only really interested in money and certainly not our welfare.

'Get out' came from our driver, and we immediately piled out of the vehicle. We stepped straight out onto a muddy patch of ground and could see that the group of people were families with kids just like us. There were children of all ages and elderly people, but they all had the same haunted expression. I realised that's what we must look like, too.

I wondered what everyone else's story was. What struggles had they gone through to get here? And what lay ahead for them, and for us? There was no way of telling. It was very possible we would all lose our lives right here in this jungle. And yet there was a sense that we were all in it together somehow. Even though we didn't know these people there was something that pulled us together. We were all going to look after each other, that much I could tell. Race, religion, colour – none of it matters when you're out of your comfort zone.

Mum, being Mum, tried to help some of the others who looked cold and hungry. Meanwhile, Hussein started trying to distract the younger children by playing the fool. He always did this – in a stressful situation he would always act the clown, putting himself out there to bring humour and make others laugh. It had always been his way of dealing with his illness, and it came in handy now.

We must have been the last family to arrive, as within a few minutes we were told to get in a line and start walking.

No talking, we just had to follow the traffickers wherever they went.

To our alarm they all carried machetes. I wondered again whether we would all be brutally murdered right here in the forest, but Hussein said they were just for cutting back the undergrowth. Sure enough, they led the way, slashing at the leaves and brambles as they walked. Everyone followed behind, and before long we started to hold each other's hands to help each other.

We walked and walked, and the traffickers stayed ahead, chopping through the thick, humid jungle with their machetes. Dad and Mum clutched onto us tightly, and every now and then Dad would give Hussein a piggyback. He was struggling, but Dad could only carry him some of the way.

As we walked, I got talking to one of the little girls in the group. She said her name was Zara, but I didn't know where she was from or how she had got here. I asked if she had any brothers or sisters. Unlike most of the other families, she seemed to be alone with her parents.

'I had a sister,' she said quietly, and shot a look at her mother.

Before I could try to make sense of this, Dad tugged at my arm. This was his subtle way of telling me to change the subject, but Zara seemed to want to talk about her sister. Before I could stop her she told me how the traffickers had 'lost her' along the way. They didn't know where she was or what had happened to her, but Zara's dad, clearly upset, explained that there were rumours that young girls were sometimes taken and sold into slavery. They'd tried to save her but they had then targeted the mum and Zara too, and he had been severely beaten.

Until that point I'd thought that our experiences had been unbearable, but meeting Zara's family put all that into perspective. I wondered what other families in this group had gone through just to get to this point.

I could tell that Dad was shocked by what he had heard. Mum too held our hands tighter, and I could tell their eyes had been opened to a new set of fears. As a family we were holding on to the promise of a 'safe haven', a bubble we had created and were willing to take risks for. But what if the risks weren't worth it? What if the 'safe haven' didn't exist? How much were we willing to sacrifice to get there?

I remember Mum reaching out and holding Zara's mum's hand without saying a word. What could we say? They would probably never see their daughter again, and we had no idea how that felt.

'God give you patience,' Dad said, giving Zara's dad a hug.

For us, leaving Herat had been a matter of life and death – both for Mum and for Hussein. But for other families, maybe they regretted taking this risk? Maybe they had no idea how inhuman some people were. Maybe the risk hadn't been worth it.

The group was subdued as the reality of our situation hit home. We marched on for what must have been several kilometres, the traffickers ahead of us the whole time. Every so often we would have to wait as the 'watcher' at the head of the group would confirm that the path was clear. Every time this happened it seemed we had to wait longer and longer, and being in the jungle was taking its toll. There were what seemed like hundreds of mosquitoes, and Hessam in particular was getting badly bitten. Mum would attempt to brush them away, but it was no use.

At the next stop, as we sat on the ground, the wait felt even longer than usual. It seemed like hours, and we were all getting tired and fed up, especially the younger children. Eventually, some of the group went ahead to see what the hold-up was, only to find that the traffickers were nowhere to be seen.

That was it, they were gone, leaving us alone in the jungle with no idea where we were or what we should do now. Dad had that worried look on his face again, and we knew we were in real trouble. Once again we had no idea what to do. What if they never came back and just left us here in the jungle? What if it started to get dark?

We had no means of transport, no food, no shelter and only the clothes we were wearing. I thought of home: the bed I shared with my brothers, the *sofra* set for dinner, the smell of lamb and saffron coming through from the kitchen. I just wanted to go back.

Mum rallied us by saying that we were a family, we were together and we were heading for a better future. We cheered up a little, and huddled together with the rest of the group. A few of the men volunteered to go ahead and see if they could see anything or anyone who might be able to help.

Mum's look at Dad said 'Don't go', and he held us tighter, his hands around our shoulders. Being separated was the worst thing that could happen, and we didn't want to risk it. Instead, Dad tried to distract us with family memories.

'Remember when Hamed fell into the big pan when he was little and we called him *digcheh*,' he said with a cheeky smile. I hated this story, and immediately rose to the bait, getting defensive.

'That's why we call you "hot head",' said Hussein cheerfully. "Cos you fell into a hot pan.' He giggled, knowing he would get a reaction from me. Suddenly we could hear someone running towards the group. Terrified, we ran for cover – behind logs, branches, anything we could find.

'They're here,' said one of the men, as they all came back through the undergrowth. Sure enough the traffickers were on their tail, thrashing through the jungle with their machetes. Who would have thought we'd be so relieved to see a bunch of strangers coming through the jungle with machetes!

They barked at us that the road ahead was blocked, and that we needed to go a different way. There was an audible groan from the children, as they knew this would mean yet more walking, but the parents chivvied them along and we set off in a slightly different direction.

After what must have been a few more hours of walking, darkness started to fall. This made the jungle even more wild and terrifying, and we were extra relieved when we finally heard the traffickers say that we were nearly there. We didn't know where 'there' was, or what was in store for us, but at least we could stop walking.

I started to visualise what would be waiting for us on the other side of this journey. Would it be any better? I was starting to lose faith. After a whole day of trekking through the jungle I just wanted a comfy bed and some food.

Instead, my heart sank as I saw yet another four-by-four ahead of us. I couldn't bear the thought of another bumpy ride. The driver pointed at the vehicle and told us to hurry up and get in. We didn't even get a chance to say goodbye to the friends we'd made in the group and I wondered what would happen to them. As we got into the car I waved to Zara and wished she could be my sister.

So there we were, back in a four-by-four, Mum clutching onto Hussein so he wouldn't hit the roof or sides. Dad was in the front seat and Hessam and I were left to bounce around in the back. The crazy driver revved the engine and we hurtled off over the bumps and hills again. After a while I started to feel sick, but soon the road became less bumpy and I wondered whether we were finally leaving the jungle.

Although I'd been concentrating on looking straight ahead so I wouldn't throw up, I dared myself to look out of the window to see where we were. The darkness of the jungle had gone, but we were still on an off-road muddy track. The driver mumbled something and then pointed ahead of him on the track. Dad leaned forward to work out what he was pointing at and then turned around to us and said, 'Get ready.'

Mum loosened here grip on Hussein and the car turned down a remote track to what looked like a farm. I could smell manure, which made me feel even more sick, and Hessam just laughed at the faces I was pulling. He started to wind me up, teasing me about cow muck, but then the driver opened the back door and told us to get out.

The first thing I saw when I jumped down from the four-by-four were farm animals. That explained the smell. A friendly-looking woman came up to us and pointed towards

the barn, ushering us across the farmyard. We suddenly realised that this was where we'd be staying for the night. Dad
told us that we weren't in Russia any more but Ukraine, a
neighbouring country, and we'd had to go through the jungle
to avoid the border.

The woman led us to the barn and opened a battered
wooden door, showing us inside our new home. Thankfully,
the smell inside the barn wasn't as bad as outside, but it was
clear the last occupants had had four legs rather than two.
As the door opened further, we saw that there was another
group of people huddled in the corner of the barn. In some
ways this was a relief – at least we weren't the only ones
using the farm for shelter.

The woman half pushed us inside and then shut the door
behind us, and we heard her pull a bolt across it from the
outside. So we were trapped in a barn, with people we didn't
know, in a country we had never been to before.

I suddenly realised how tired I was after such a long day
walking, and we found a spot that looked comfortable and lay
down to sleep while Dad inspected the barn.

I could hear Dad talking with one of the men from the
other group, and Mum was checking on Hussein. Hessam
was already asleep, but I couldn't go to sleep as I was too
interested in the barn and what was outside. I found some
holes in the wall where the material had rotted, and I peered
outside. I could make out some horses in a field and I wondered if there would be a black one. I liked black horses the
best – they always seemed so strong and powerful.

'Can I have a black horse one day?' I whispered to Mum,
who was cradling a sleeping Hessam in her lap. I cuddled up

next to her and she started stroking my hair. I could imagine myself riding that black horse, feeling tough and strong and in charge of everything. I'd like a white one too though, for the times when I want to be peaceful. *Today I want to be peaceful,* I thought, as I drifted off to sleep.

The next morning we woke to the sound of animal noises. Hessam was still asleep so we chatted to Dad about where we were. He said that the other group told him they'd only been there for a day, which he thought was a good sign. Hopefully we'd soon be out of here.

Next, we needed some breakfast. Dad banged loudly on the bolted wooden door several times until the woman who shut us in the day before opened it.

'Do you have anything to eat for the kids?' said Dad in Russian, but the lady who now looked stone-faced just stared at him. Then she said 'Dollars.'

Dad reached into his secret pocket and pulled out a few dollars, but before he could even hand them over the woman snatched them out of this hand and slammed the door. Hessam, who had been woken by the banging, looked like he was trying not to cry.

We rushed away from the door and I took up my position at the rotten hole again, hoping I'd be able to see the woman returning with some food. We were starving, and pushed and jostled each other to see out of the hole. After what seemed like ages the grumpy lady finally came out holding something. We ran to the barn door and she opened it and half threw in some stale bread and what seemed like homemade cheese, which was squishy and had a rotten taste. It was probably the worst breakfast we'd ever had, but we were so hungry we didn't care.

# CHAPTER 7

# James and John

We spent a few days in the barn, having only stale bread and the soft cheese to eat, until we were told it was once again time to move on. We were strangely excited, but I could tell Mum was getting fed up with the constant moving and not being able to give us enough food. Hussein was starting to show signs of getting worse after all the travelling and the poor diet, and I could tell she was worried about him.

The morning we were due to leave, Hessam started to complain that his back hurt. I found this hilarious, and teased him terribly, poking him and running away. The more Hessam whinged and scratched the harder I laughed, until Dad came to take a look. As soon as he got close he flinched and called Mum over. 'That's more than just an itch,' he said.

Mum, looking horrified, distracted Hessam while Dad tried to look more closely. Suddenly Hessam screamed out in pain, and I stopped laughing. Dad held up what he'd found under Hessam's skin. 'What is *that?*' we all cried. 'Larvae,' replied Dad. 'They're underneath the skin.'

I certainly wasn't laughing now, wondering if anything like that was lurking under the skin on my backside.

Once we had all calmed down, the 'Poop Lady', as Hussein had christened her due to the smell of our surroundings, came to the barn to tell us our transport had arrived.

The transport was a car, which slowed down as it entered the farmyard. Inside was an elderly couple, waving frantically at us. 'Do we know them?' Hussein asked, confused.

'Not that I know of,' said Dad. 'Perhaps they just like giving value for money.'

Again, the lady told Dad to sit in the front, while the rest of us had to get into another secret compartment in the back seat. As Hessam and I fought for the best space, Hussein seemed quiet. When Mum asked, he said that he was tired, but I knew from the look on his face that his heart was having a funny turn. I didn't say anything to Mum, as there was nothing we could do anyway, and it would only have worried her.

'I just need Hamed to move his fat ass,' he said, putting on a brave face, and I immediately came back with an insult. There was no point making the situation even more complicated.

We drove for hours through the night, with toilet stops few and far between. The elderly couple took turns driving and buildings turned to fields as the countryside got more and more remote.

We were sick of car rides by the time the car came to a stop. We were once again by what looked like a block of apartments, but this time it didn't look as scary as Moscow.

'Where are we, Dad?' said Hussein, his face hopeful.

Dad asked the couple in broken Russian where we were and, after a slight pause, they mumbled a city name which we didn't recognise. Dad obviously didn't either, and just said 'We'll be there soon, son, I promise.'

My parents always knew that any sudden rush of emotions could trigger Hussein's heart palpitations, so everything had to be carefully messaged. Whether it was good news or bad, they would always quietly reassure him. But Hussein knew they had no idea where we were or where we were going. We all knew that. What Mum and Dad didn't realise was that Hussein had the ability to be hopeful in any situation. He always found the positive and focused his energy on that.

We all got out of the car and headed to our new home. At least it was a building with a roof. And at least it wasn't as cold as Moscow.

While Dad was talking to the couple to try to find out what our next move would be, we made our way towards the apartment. I wondered if there was a TV. And if there were rats. But in truth I didn't really care. I just wanted somewhere to lie down and go to sleep.

As the couple let us into the apartment the first thing we noticed was that it was all green. Green carpet, green curtains, green walls ... but apart from that it seemed okay. It wouldn't be that bad if we had to stay here for a while.

That night we managed a small meal round the little table in the kitchen. While we had no idea where we were or where we'd be heading from here, at that moment, it didn't seem to matter. As we ate, Hussein put one hand on my shoulder and one on Hessam's and whispered, 'Brothers forever.' We nodded. I loved that smile.

We slept okay in the little apartment, and in the morning we sat round the little table again. Before we knew it, we got a call to say we would be moving on. Dad put the phone down to tell us that we had to be ready in just a few hours. Our mystery stay in this mystery country was over.

Of course, there wasn't anything to get ready. We had no clothes, no suitcases to pack, so we just passed the hours watching foreign-language TV in the apartment. All we had could be put into a small bag which one of us wore on our back in case there was trouble and we needed to run, but we had learnt to prepare ourselves mentally for what was ahead. We had learnt to think like adults and act as a unit, not as individuals.

After a few hours the doorbell rang and Mum jumped. Dad opened the door and greeted the handler, who seemed to be more important than others we'd met. He wore a leather jacket and jeans, and in the back pocket was a handgun he called his 'baby'. I'd seen guns before, but never a little handgun like this. This was like in a movie.

Mum tried to pull me away, but I was fascinated. As the handler talked to Dad about the plans for getting away, I kept staring at the gun.

'Want to see it?' asked the handler finally. 'C'mon, have a look. It's even got my name on it,' he said as he called me over.

Mum tried to hold on to me, but I was mesmerised and went over. I stuck my hand out and the handler put the gun in my palm.

'Don't worry, the safety is on,' he said to Mum.

So I got to hold the gun for a few minutes while Dad talked to the handler about our future plans. Eventually he beckoned me over with a smile, and I walked gingerly towards him, still holding the gun. He took it off me and Mum looked relieved.

'*Spasibo*, John,' he said as he took the gun away. John? That wasn't my name. Why was he calling me John? Mum and Dad looked confused too, and he smiled.

'Yes,' he said, then pointing at Hessam, 'and that one's James. These are your new names.'

He laughed, putting the gun back in his back pocket. Then he reached inside the pocket of his leather jacket and brought out some shiny passports, handing them to Dad. As Dad opened one of them the penny dropped.

'Fake passports?' he asked.

'Yes,' said the handler. 'If the country where you are going to knows where you have come from, they will deport you straight back there. These are just to get you through security this side and help you get to the UK.'

My ears pricked up. The UK? Was that where we were heading?

'But how are we supposed to pretend to be British?' said Dad. 'We can't speak English.'

The handler didn't seem to think this was a problem and proceeded to teach us some words in his own broken English. He made us repeat after him: 'hello', 'bye', 'thank you'.

We were excited at our new knowledge, and ran round the apartment calling each other John and saying 'Bye! Thank you!' on a loop. The handler went on discussing plans with Dad for a few moments, then he left, telling us he would come back to collect us in a few hours.

'Goodbye and thank you,' Mum whispered towards the door as Dad shut up the apartment and we went down the stairs. We knew there were some families that weren't as fortunate as us, whose journey had been more dangerous, so we were always thankful for a safe place to stay.

We stepped out into the street and saw the handler waiting by his car. Dad ushered us towards it and we went to the boot. But this time the back door was opened for us. We were allowed to sit in the back! Dad nodded to us, and we realised that this was part of the plan. People with passports don't hide in secret compartments in the boot.

We fastened our seatbelts and the car started up. We drove through the unknown city until the streets became a dual carriageway with many different lanes. After we had been driving for just a few minutes we suddenly came to a police checkpoint. My heart was racing, but the policeman just gave the handler a nod and waved us through.

'Is he mafia?' whispered Hussein to Mum through a fake smile. Mum just looked ahead.

My imagination was running wild in the back seat. Who was this man? Was he mafia, or maybe a corrupt police officer? Whoever he was, no one seemed to stand in his way.

Eventually the car slowed down as we approached what

looked like an airport. 'Are we going to fly?' we all whispered to Mum at once. I'd never been on a plane.

'I don't know,' she said, and shushed us. Hussein was quiet and pale, and I could see she was worried about him, but there was no time to make a fuss.

We stopped and were told to get out of the car. Mum held on to Hussein as we stepped onto the tarmac and Dad and the handler called him over.

After speaking with them briefly Hussein came back to us with a grin on his face. What was funny? To our surprise he opened the top of his trousers and revealed Mum and Dad's real Afghan passports – the *Tazkira* – shoved down his pants. We burst out laughing and looked over at Dad in disbelief. Dad shrugged. 'What?' he grinned. 'We need somewhere safe to keep them until we get to the safe haven!'

With a few final instructions from the handler, we made our way into the airport. We were to use the fake passports to get through security and on to the plane and keep the *Tazkira* hidden. Then, once we were safely through, we would dispose of the fake passports and keep the *Tazkira* to prove who we really were and be able to seek asylum. If anything went wrong we would be caught and deported, or maybe even imprisoned. There would be no escape.

Hessam and I fidgeted terribly as we made our way through the airport, Mum holding on to our hands while Dad held Hussein. The first stop was the passport check. There were no hiccups, except I was so nervous I kept saying 'hello, hello' to everyone I saw. It was the only word I could remember.

Next was the security check. Hussein looked a bit clammy as we approached, but Dad nodded at us to say that everything would be okay. Would it? How did he know? What if they found the passports down Hussein's trousers?

The security guards started patting Hussein down, and I worried that his heart wouldn't cope with all the stress. That would certainly draw attention to us. I could see him trying to breathe regularly, while at the same time smiling and saying 'hello'.

Then suddenly there was a beeping sound. That was it. We were caught. We'd be back in Afghanistan and Mum would be killed. I couldn't control my panic as the security guards started scanning for metal round Hussein's body.

BEEP, BEEP BEEEEEP the scanner went, and the security guard pointed to Hussein's trousers. There was no point creating a distraction now, we were done for.

'It's okay, you can go,' the security guard said suddenly.

Hussein looked confused. Dad looked at him as if to say 'Just go!' and Hussein moved out of the security area.

'It must have been your belt,' Dad said when we were out of ear shot. 'As soon as the guard saw it he seemed happy enough to let you go. An inch lower and he would have come across the passports!'

Mum looked exhausted. The close call had made us all jumpy, and I realised what a strain all of this was putting on her. Not to mention her worries about Hussein.

Suddenly we were heading towards the gate and about to fly in a real-life aeroplane for the first time. I couldn't believe it. We looked out of the huge windows and wondered which of the enormous planes would be ours. Dad shook his head and pointed to a smaller aircraft that looked like a private plane. 'That's ours.'

'That one?' said Hussein. 'How's Hamed's fat ass going to fit on that?' We all laughed.

As we got on the plane there were no hidden compartments this time. There were huge leather seats – plenty of room for all of us to stretch out. As we started to lift into the sky my stomach felt strange – it was a sensation I had never experienced before and it made me nervous. But once we'd taken off, one by one we fell asleep next to Mum. Even though we had no idea where we were going, and we were up among the clouds in such a small plane, we felt safer than we had in days.

After what felt like only a few minutes I could feel Mum shaking me awake. 'Wake up, sleepy head,' she said, as the plane started to dip down to land. We could see green fields below, and wherever it was looked pretty safe to me. I wondered if it was England. I hoped so. Then Hussein could get better.

Dad called me over. 'I've got a job for you when we land,' he said. I suddenly felt important.

'What?'

The plane rumbled and tumbled towards the runway as Dad explained that when we landed we would need to get rid of the fake passports. And I was in charge.

As we took our things and stepped down from the plane, I was already formulating a plan. We walked out onto the tarmac from the luxury plane. It was hard to imagine that just a few hours earlier we'd been sleeping in a barn.

'Okay, stick together, boys,' instructed Dad, handing me the passports.

'Why are you giving them to Hamed?' asked Hussein. 'He'll only lose them.' Hessam also looked puzzled.

'It's okay,' I said. 'Dad just wants me to do something.' This was my moment. There was no way anyone was going to take this job from me.

'Let's just wait here,' said Dad, and I took this as my cue. I wandered off, the passports tucked safely into my jumper.

I walked through the airport terminal. There were people everywhere: families, luggage, businessmen. There were also airport staff. All I had to do was get rid of the passports so they couldn't be traced back to us. I just had to find the toilets.

Eventually I saw a gentlemen sign on one of the back walls. I sauntered towards it. My plan was simple: I'd lock myself in, rip each page into shreds and flush them away.

I went into the toilets and found an empty cubicle. My palms sweating, I locked the door behind me and started to rip the pages one by one. I knew that Mum and Dad would be waiting nervously outside and Hussein and Hessam would be asking where I was. But I had to make sure everything to do with John and James disappeared down the toilet.

I was flushing pages away a few at a time. Everything was going okay – until I got to the covers. They were tougher than the inside pages and I couldn't rip them. They weren't made of paper, but a sort of thick leather. Impatiently, I chucked them into the toilet and flushed. The water cleared. They were still there. So I flushed again, waiting impatiently for the cistern to fill up. Still they wouldn't go down the toilet.

Anyone inside the toilets at that point would be wondering why I was flushing so many times. But the passport covers just wouldn't go down. What was I going to do? If I didn't destroy the passports someone might find them and trace them back to us. More importantly, I would have failed at the one job Dad had asked me to do.

I decided that drastic times called for drastic measures, so I looked around the cubicle for something that might help me work out what to do. I glanced down at my worn brown boots. Got it.

I lifted my leg and stuck my boot down the toilet as far as it would go, pushing the passport covers down into the water. Still they didn't go. The tip of my boot was too big for the u-bend in the toilet and all I succeeded in doing was getting a wet foot.

Mum and Dad would be worrying by now. The only thing to do was to leave the cubicle and go back to them to see what they wanted me to do.

My right boot was stained dark with water as I walked back through the terminal to where the others were waiting. Would what I'd done be good enough?

Hussein and Hessam stared at my wet boot as I whispered the problem in Dad's ear. He shook his head. It was no good. I had to get rid of the passports without a trace, otherwise the guards could find out who we were and how we'd got here. I had to go back and try again.

I rushed back to the toilets. This time I was determined to finish my task. If I had to use my hands, I thought, I would.

I got back into the toilets and counted – one, two, three doors from the left – there was the cubicle I'd been in. I pushed the door. Someone was in there! Panicking, I stood back by the sinks and waited, trying not to draw attention to myself. Just as I was wondering what I was going to tell Dad, the door to the cubicle opened. I rushed in – and realised that it was the wrong one.

I wandered back out of the cubicle and waited. By now there was a queue of people behind me, and the person next in line was wondering why I wasn't going in. I smiled and gestured at the door, telling the guy next in the queue to go in before me. There was nothing else for it – I'd just have to wait until the right cubicle was free.

Minutes passed, and each time another cubicle became free I smiled and let the person behind me go in it. What was happening in my cubicle? Why wouldn't the person come out? And how long before people thought I was up to something, letting everyone go before me in a queue of people?

Finally, the right door opened. But the person who'd been in there all that time wasn't a passenger. It was an airport security guard. My stomach dropped. He must have seen the cover pages of the passports and that's why he was so long! We were done for.

My mind racing, I slipped past the security guard and into the toilet. Then it hit me. The reason he was so long in that cubicle wasn't because of our passports – it was because of his lunch. A quick glance down the toilet and I could see that the passports had definitely vanished. Without wasting another second I rushed out of the toilets to find Dad.

'It's done,' I panted, when I finally saw him.

'Definitely?' he asked.

'Definitely,' I said. 'And I don't think anyone will go in there for a while.'

Now that we'd got rid of the fake passports we had to wait in arrivals until it was safe to go through passport control. Dad said the mafia guy told him we should wait at least a few hours, as that way they'd be less likely to track where we'd come from. If they found out which flight we'd come in on they could just send us straight back. Which would be interesting, because we didn't even know where that was ourselves.

When enough time had passed, we were to go through passport control. At this point the authorities would see we had no documents and officially declare us refugees. The mafia guy had taught us all how to say the word in English. From that point on, Dad said, people would view us differently. We wouldn't be the Amiri family any more; we wouldn't even be James or John. We'd be invisible: a number, a statistic on a spreadsheet. That's what the word 'refugee' did to people.

Despite Dad's doom and gloom, we were impatient. 'How much longer?' I pestered. Once we'd ridden the escalators a few times and looked at all the vending machines, the airport was boring. Mum and Dad tried to sleep on the uncomfortable plastic airport chairs and we watched people come and go.

'A few more hours, just to be safe,' Dad muttered.

Mum told us to stay close by. Even in an airport she was worried we'd get into danger. She was always trying to protect us – especially Hussein, but we were pretty savvy by now. We were a team.

After a few more hours, Dad called us over and said, 'It's time'. Dad said this a lot. It meant that something was going to change, but we didn't know what. It could be better or worse, but it was always different.

We took our bag and queued up at the little glass cubicle. A grumpy-looking passport guard called people one by one to show their passports, and as each person handed over their documents he would look up and stare at them, matching their face with the photo in the passport. Sometimes he would ask a few questions before waving them through.

We stood in line nervously. We had no passports other than the *Tazkira*, no photos and no documents. All we had was that word: refugee.

'Next,' called grumpy man. Dad seemed nervous, although he was trying to hide it. We approached the glass.

The man seemed annoyed that we'd come in a group. 'Only one at a time,' he said. 'Passport.' He stared out at us. Dad took a breath and shook his head slowly. Grumpy man just stared. Dad shook his head again and held up his hands as if to say 'no passport'. Then, in his best but broken English, he said the word he'd been told to say, the word that would change our lives forever: 'Refugee.'

# CHAPTER 8

# 'Refugee'

For a minute, the man in the cubicle didn't say anything. Then, after a while, we started to wonder whether Dad had said the right word after all. What if 'refugee' meant something else? What if the handler had been pulling our leg? Dad raised his voice and said it again: 'Refugee.'

The grumpy man shifted, then broke his stare and called over one of his colleagues. After a short conversation with them, he turned to us.

He said something to us in English, but we couldn't understand him. Then we realised he was pointing towards a set of chairs in a corner of the airport terminal, and we presumed he wanted us to sit there.

I was surprised. Shouldn't we be arrested or something? Was that all we had to do – sit down? Dad, still not knowing whether they'd understood him correctly, said 'Refugee' again, this time looking into the grumpy man's eyes to see if he understood. 'Refugee. Refugee,' he said. The grumpy man nodded. 'Yes, sit down please.'

We could feel the eyes of everyone in the airport on us as we walked over to the chairs. We knew we didn't belong here, but where did we belong? What's a family supposed to do when it has nowhere safe to go?

We see people every day and we don't know their story. We don't know why they do things, or what they're running from. What do we know about what's happened to complete strangers? None of those people staring at us in that airport knew why we'd left our home and family behind. Did they think we wanted to sit, embarrassed, on those plastic airport chairs? Dad was right: 'refugee' changed everything.

After we'd waited for a little while we noticed that grumpy man was talking to someone else at the glass counter. He was pointing to the plastic chairs again. Then more people came, and he pointed them to the chairs as well. One by one they all came over to where we were sitting and sat with us.

The longer we waited the more they came, and after a while we were surrounded by others, who must have been refugees too. It was as if they'd been waiting for us to get there first.

Eventually there weren't any more people, and we started to wonder what was going to happen to us all. Then a guard came over. He called us into a side room, and again Mum told us to stay close. I think one of the things she was most scared of was us being separated from each other. Back in Afghanistan we'd always been taught to stick together, so it

wasn't like we were going to split up. But Mum must have
known something we didn't, because as soon as we got near
the waiting room the guards took Dad aside, gesturing to
another door.

'Look after them,' Dad managed to say to Mum as he was
taken away, as if he needed to tell her. Then he added, 'Keep
telling them Hussein needs medical attention.'

We went into the side room and sat down. Mum cried.
Thankfully, after only a few minutes Dad was allowed back
in to join us.

'I think they're fetching a translator,' he said. He told us
that the man had spoken to him in German a lot, and all he
knew was that his name was Lukas. Dad had managed to tell
him that our name was Amiri, that we were from Afghanistan
and we spoke Farsi. After that Lukas had brought him back
to us and left.

'He seems to want to help,' said Dad. 'And he seemed to
understand that I'd want to come and wait with you.'

We realised it might be a while before they could fetch
a translator, but before long Lukas came into the room with
some water and food for us. As he gave it to Dad he said
something in German. Dad smiled. When he'd gone, we
asked Dad what he'd said.

'No idea,' Dad said. 'But it sounded kind. I think he's on
our side.' Maybe we were going to be okay after all. It would
be a first – the only people who'd helped us since we'd left
Afghanistan were people we'd paid.

We waited some more, and I watched as Hussein fell
asleep on Mum's shoulder. His mouth opened and he started
to dribble. I nudged Hessam and we giggled. Hussein had

looked paler and more unwell these last few weeks. He looked thin too, but I guess we all did. He never seemed ill, but I knew he did a good job of hiding it when his heart played up, so who knew how he was doing really? I started to daydream about finding somewhere new to live, somewhere that was not only safe but where Hussein could get better.

I was about to fall asleep when suddenly Lukas came back into the room, smiling. Mum shook Hussein awake.

The translator had arrived. Lukas brought him in, but before he could say anything, Dad turned to him and said in Farsi, 'Can you do me a favour please? Can you thank him from me and my family?' He pointed at Lukas.

The translator nodded. '*Er möchte dir danken,*' he said to Lukas.

Lukas smiled again, then took Dad's hand and shook it. I thought he was probably a dad too.

With that out of the way Dad started talking quickly at the translator, explaining everything about our situation and where we'd come from. Suddenly he stopped. 'We don't even know where we are,' he said.

The translator smiled and said, 'You're in Austria.'

A huge smile spread across Mum and Dad's faces. What was so good about Austria? Whatever it was, they seemed pretty pleased about being here. Maybe it was because we were in Europe. The UK was in Europe.

I always wondered why Mum and Dad were so set on living in the UK. Surely anywhere in Europe would have done? Yes, back home everyone thought of the UK as somewhere safe, somewhere we'd be welcome. But it wasn't until later that I found out the UK had the best healthcare system for Hussein, somewhere he could get the operation he needed.

Finally, after what felt like hours, the questions and talking were over and it was time for us to leave. But where were we going? As we were escorted out of the airport to a waiting van Dad told us what was next: 'We're being transferred to a refugee camp.'

'What's a refugee camp like?' I asked.

'I haven't the faintest idea.'

As we got into the van, it still felt strange not to have to hide in the boot. We pressed our faces up against the windows, looking out at the greenery shooting by as we sped down the motorway. Travelling in daylight was a novelty for us too, and there was so much to see.

'Where's the refugee camp?' asked Hessam suddenly.

'Don't worry,' said Dad, 'it will be safe.'

'Safe' was the word we'd been running on for months. Was 'safe' actually happening now? I could definitely sense Mum's tension dropping as we sat in the back of the van heading down the motorway. We hadn't felt safe for so long. It was like we'd made a bubble around us, and inside it we'd stuck together. Even growing up in Herat, I'd never realised how much I'd taken safety for granted.

As I looked out of the window at the fields and hedges, I wondered what our home in the UK was going to be like. Would we be able to sleep and eat in peace? Right now, that was all I wanted: to stay in one place for a while and not feel like we were always being made to move on. I looked at Hussein. Time was running out for him. We all knew that.

The van slowed down as it reach a security barrier. Behind it we could see buildings and a huge open area, like a campus. There were people of all ages – families, old people, children and teenagers – milling around in groups. But in the background I could see something else, something I'd only ever seen on TV. It was a football field.

I couldn't believe it. After all this time, this was waiting here for us? You could forget the UK. This place was where I wanted to be. It was like heaven: not only would we have a roof over our head and food in our tummies, but we had a playing field out the back.

I thought back to the families we'd trekked through the jungle with. Had they made it to somewhere like this? Had Zara and her family found a camp like this one? Or were they still on the road?

I was still taking in the amazingness of our new home when the van stopped and we were told to get out. We all breathed in the air as if we'd been holding our breath for months. I didn't care what the future held – as long as we could stay here.

Although Hussein and I were itching to get on that playing field, we had some more waiting to do. First there were all the checks that had to be made on new families, and then it seemed to take them a long time to work out which part of the huge camp we were supposed to go to. There were lots of questions. Then we had to wait some more until they brought us some towels, toiletries and toothpaste.

Finally we were allowed out. We raced around that playing field until our legs hurt. That night, eating dinner almost felt like normal. The weather was warm, and the table was outside, so we all sat and looked at the dark sky as we ate. I was a bit proud of us for getting here. We'd worked as a team. All the horrible things that had happened had just brought us closer together, and I felt like there was nothing we couldn't do. Yes, there had been a few close calls, and some other times when we'd been really lucky, but this just made me think there really must be someone up there looking after us.

I wasn't stupid. I knew that the tough times weren't over and that this couldn't last forever. But I didn't want to think about that right now. I just wanted to lock this moment in my head and never let it end. It had felt so long since we'd been somewhere nice that I wanted to remember that feeling forever.

As we fell asleep that night the moon came down through the little windows of the room and I slept well for the first time in ages. In fact, I slept so deeply that I could hardly bear to get up the next morning.

I was still sleepy when Mum came to tell us to get dressed. This wasn't a holiday camp, she said, and breakfast wouldn't last all morning.

At this we all started to move. It was a long time since we'd had a proper breakfast. We made our way to a large hall and got in line. Seeing the crowds of other families, we realised for the first time how big the camp was. Then suddenly, among all the chatter, we could hear people talking in our own language, and I had a sudden pang of longing for home. Were some of the other families here from Afghanistan too? Dad went over to say hi and Mum started to chat to some of the other Afghan women. We tried to make friends too, but the other children were much quieter than us and didn't seem to want to play.

That first full day was amazing. We played with some of the other kids on the field, while Mum and Dad drank tea outside, and before we knew it the sky was getting dark. Mum still watched us closely, but they seemed more relaxed now we were surrounded by people who could speak our language.

Over the next few days we had the same routine: breakfast in the morning followed by chores in our room, then football until lunch. After lunch we would play some more until the sun went down and it was time for the evening meal. Then Mum and Dad would drink tea with the other Afghans until they called us in to bed. I could have stayed in that camp forever. But we also knew that we didn't have time on our hands, and Hussein was getting weaker every day. Somehow, we had to press on and try to get to the UK – we couldn't leave it in the hands of the Austrian authorities. As much as we all wanted to spend some time at the camp recovering, we couldn't forget that we were still on a journey. And we still had a long way to go.

# CHAPTER 9

# Box Boy

In our journey so far, we always knew when we were about to move on, as Dad would start to make calls. He said this part of the journey would be more straightforward. We just had to get from Austria into Germany and from there we could try to find a way into the UK. In fact, he said, the next part of the journey wouldn't be difficult at all – it would be luxury. Excited about not having to hide in boots or be thrown around in a four-by-four, we waited impatiently for moving day. Little did we know what was to come.

When the day arrived, Dad got a call from the handler and it was time to say goodbye to our little slice of heaven. I'd never been so sad to leave anywhere in my life. We'd had fun, freedom and – most importantly – football. I'd also made some good friends. But we all knew it wasn't permanent, and it wasn't going to make Hussein better.

The camp gates were always left open during the day, so after leaving our room we waited at the entrance. After a while a car pulled up. It was a Mercedes! Dad wasn't wrong about it being luxury. The driver called us over and told us to get in.

I gave a quick glance back at the camp. 'Don't you want to say goodbye to your friends, Hamed?' Mum said. I shook my head.

'No. It's time to go.'

Mum knew not to push it. I didn't want to think too much about what I was leaving behind. It wasn't the first time I'd lost friends, and it probably wouldn't be the last. We had to get going, so there was no point feeling sad about what we'd left. It was how I coped. I guess I wasn't like other boys of eleven.

Within a few minutes of being on the road the camp felt like a distant memory. We were used to moving on, so I started to think of what lay ahead. I could hear Mum praying under her breath, like she always did when we moved from one place to another.

Before we knew it the city became one long road. Then this road turned into a wide motorway with lots of lanes. We were going so fast the white lines on the road began to look like a blur. I'd never been in a car driving that fast before. I was scared, but I liked it at the same time.

'What's the rush?' Dad asked the driver.

'No rush,' he said mysteriously. 'Just testing the speed of the car.'

I felt the mood in the car change, and looked at Mum. She was nervous, and I could see her trying to catch Dad's eye. Something was wrong.

'We're now entering Germany,' smiled the driver. This was good news. Wasn't it? I could feel Mum's grip on me getting tighter and tighter, and soon Hussein noticed it too. I looked at Dad. He also looked a bit uneasy, and I could tell he knew Mum's hackles were up.

I stayed glued to the window, watching the autobahn whizz past. Were we being kidnapped? Even if we were, what could we do about it? We just had to wait and see where the driver took us.

Suddenly the car slowed and we started to pull in at the next stop. 'We need to get fuel,' the driver said. But I could see he had at least half a tank left. It didn't add up.

Dad looked quickly at Mum, and by now we all knew something was wrong. I nudged Hussein and gave him a look. It meant 'be ready for anything'.

'We're here,' said the driver. Where? I didn't understand. This was just a service station, and it was in the middle of nowhere. There was something about the way the driver spoke that gave me the creeps too.

Then he turned to us and said, 'Please don't do anything and give me all your money.' He was pointing something at Dad, who was sitting in the seat next to him. Straight away I could see that it was a gun.

My stomach dropped. Was there any way I could distract him? I looked at Dad to see if I could get a sign from him, but he quickly shook his head at me as if to say no. We were in a locked car. Even I knew we had to pick our battles.

'Okay, okay, just don't hurt my family,' said Dad. He reached for our money – what we had left of it – and then pointed at Mum's bag. He didn't want the driver turning on her too. Mum emptied it out.

The driver took the money and put it away. 'I was told "Germany". So here you are!' he said cheerfully. Then he opened the doors, pushed us out onto the tarmac and slammed them shut.

We picked ourselves up, Dad furious and Mum fussing around to make sure we were okay. She was shaking with fear. I just wanted to get us as far away from that man and his gun as possible.

As we hurried away from the car I turned back and saw the driver put the gun back in his jacket, spin his wheels and then speed off.

So there we were, once again stranded in the middle of nowhere.

Mum fussed around Hussein. This was just the kind of thing that could trigger an episode.

'Mum, I'm okay,' Hussein said. 'I'm fine. Are you okay?'

Mum nodded. But we weren't okay. For the second time we were in the middle of nowhere in a foreign country and all our money had been stolen.

Once we'd calmed down and made sure Hussein was okay, it was time to work out what to do. We knew we were in Germany, but we had no idea how to get to where we were supposed to be. We had no money to make any calls and couldn't walk anywhere because we were at a service station on the motorway. What were we going to do?

Suddenly I remembered something. I reached into my pockets and pulled out some loose change. 'Dad, I have some change from the camp. Would that help?'

Dad smiled. 'It might.' But who would we call? We knew no one in Germany, and who could we ask to help us, thousands of miles from home?

Dad got a piece of paper out of his pocket and started to look at it. It was his list of names and numbers: friends, family and acquaintances he could contact in case we ran into trouble. Most of them I'd never heard of – they were extended family who'd moved to Europe years ago – but I knew that if they were family they'd help.

'We might be in luck,' Dad said. He looked around for a payphone.

Mum took us to the side of the service station to wait while Dad rushed inside with my loose change. She prayed quietly. We'd got this far I suppose, so maybe her prayers were working.

Sure enough, a few minutes later Dad rushed back. He was smiling. Mum raised her eyes to the sky in thanks and we all crowded round him.

'We're going to have to sit tight, but a very old friend of mine is going to pick us up,' he said. He grinned with relief.

It turned out we had to 'sit tight' for hours. We spent the time counting cars and watching in amazement at how fast they were going on the autobahn. Each time one of them pulled into the service station we wondered if it was our ride, but each time they drove past us. Eventually, a car pulled in and the driver waved towards Dad.

'That's us,' Dad said. We traipsed towards the car. We must have been a pathetic sight. We had no money, nowhere to stay and no idea where we really were. We were trusting this person to take us somewhere safe.

It was a long journey. Unlike the Mercedes this was no luxury car. After what seemed like hours we came to a town, and we were driven to a little apartment owned by Dad's contact. 'You can stay here for a few days,' he told us, in Farsi.

Dad looked relieved. He shook the man's hand. 'That means such a lot to us, thank you. I owe you one,' he said. The man looked at him.

'You still have to pay rent,' he said. Dad's face fell. How were we supposed to do that? We had no money in the world, and no way to get hold of any.

But Dad said, 'Of course,' and promised that we'd pay rent somehow. After all, this man had got us out of a very tight situation.

'Great, I'll come back tomorrow and we'll discuss how. Get some sleep for now,' he said, looking at us boys.

It was a bit of a depressing night. Although we were safe – and had survived an armed robbery – we felt no closer to getting where we needed to be. And now we had to work out how to pay rent.

We searched the fridge to see if there was anything to eat and found some old cheese and butter. We were used to eating what we could find by now, so this didn't worry us.

'Let's feast,' said Hussein sarcastically, and we all sat down. Suddenly Dad stopped.

'I've had an idea,' he said.

'What is it?' asked Mum.

'I think I know how we can pay the rent.'

It was hard to sleep that night. We were so near to where we were trying to be, but I couldn't see how we were going to get enough money to get to the UK. What was Dad's idea?

How long were we going to stay here? I tried to remember the names of some of the cars we'd seen on the autobahn and the strange German words we'd overheard, and after a while I drifted off to sleep.

Breakfast was the same old cheese and butter as we'd had for dinner, and as soon as we'd finished there was a knock at the door. Dad's friend from the day before came in.

Before Dad could say anything, his friend turned to us and said, 'I've had an idea about how you can pay the rent. You can all work in my takeaway.'

Dad smiled in response. 'Great minds,' he said. 'I was going to suggest that myself.'

Hussein and I looked at each other. 'You do know we're kids, right?' I said. I wasn't sure I was ready to get a job.

'It's okay,' said Dad's friend. 'You can work at the back making pizza boxes.'

'Yeah, Box Boy,' teased Hussein. I wasn't laughing – building takeaway boxes wasn't my idea of fun. But I also knew we didn't have much choice. We all had to do things we didn't like to get to the UK. Box Boy it would be.

When we were ready, we got into Dad's friend's car and he drove us to a small takeaway shop. We got straight to work: Mum, Dad and Hussein in the kitchen making dough and Hessam and me in the back putting together the cardboard boxes.

I thought about other kids our age, normal kids. They were probably outside playing football. But we weren't normal kids, and there was nothing normal about our situation. The main thing was not to make Mum and Dad feel guilty.

At seven, Hessam was pretty rubbish at making the boxes, but I tried to up his game by challenging him to a competition and we soon got into it. Dad and Hussein were having a contest of their own, seeing who could make the dough the fastest. That's one thing you could say for our family – we never let a bad day get the better of us.

My first experience of the world of work wasn't great. For a start, I hadn't realised just how long our 'shift' would be. When, fifteen hours later, we finally finished, we were tired and grumpy. We did get some pizza though: made from Mum's dough and Hussein's choice of topping, and we sat outside the back door of the shop to enjoy it.

Little did we know how sick of pizza we'd become over the next few weeks. Each day we'd work a fifteen-hour shift to earn back the money we'd had stolen and pay Dad's friend his rent. And each day it would be pizza for lunch and pizza for dinner. Some days we even tried eating salad just to escape the never-ending pizza. If we hadn't had each other it would have been a nightmare, but we were a good team with a goal in sight, so we just got on with it.

Dad said we'd have to work in the takeaway until we got a call from a handler. Then we could move on and try to get to the UK. In the meantime, we repaid our debt and saved as much money as we could. And after several weeks it was finally time.

Dad got a call one night to say we had to get ready. Once again, we had no idea where we were going or what would happen. But at least there wouldn't be any pizza.

On the day of the move we packed our stuff as usual, but it seemed to be getting smaller and smaller. Then we went to bed early. Crammed into one bed, Hussein lay next to me in the darkness. Hessam snored nearby.

'Do you think it'll be good – in the UK?' I said.

'Depends what you mean by good,' replied Hussein.

'I don't know … fun?'

'We don't need fun,' he answered. 'We just need to stay alive.'

There was a pause. Then he added, 'Maybe it'll just be normal. That would be good.'

# CHAPTER 10

# Belgian border control

The next morning we packed our bag and stood ready by the door. I was just preparing myself for another long car journey when Dad said we had something different in store. This time, he said, we'd be travelling by train.

We were excited, but Mum wasn't too pleased. She hated trains. I was just glad we didn't have to get on the motorway again. After all, our last experience hadn't exactly ended well.

As we left the apartment Hussein nudged me. 'What's next? Camel?'

We arrived at the train station and the handler told us the journey should be simple – we'd travel by train into Belgium and then into the Netherlands, where his 'friend' would be expecting us. All we had to do was sit on the train, show our tickets and keep a low profile.

How wrong he was.

We got onto the train and found some seats as far away from other people as possible. The train was very modern, with smooth and comfortable seats. Dad said we just had to keep our heads down and it would be fine.

We spent the next few hours watching out of the window and wondering how fast we were going. Mum felt sick and wasn't enjoying it at all. At one point the conductor came and asked to see our tickets, but then he went away again. All was going to plan.

Then we came to the Belgian border. We stopped at the station for longer than we had at the others, and Dad said he could see border control getting on the train. We knew we had no passports or other documents, and offering a bribe wouldn't get us very far in Belgium. We'd just have to try and stay out of sight.

'Close your eyes and pretend you're asleep,' Dad whispered. So we did as we were told and pretended to sleep as the police moved through the compartments asking for ID. It was hard not to peep, especially as I could hear the guards getting closer.

'*Pass bitte?*' they were saying, '*Pass bitte?*' Then there'd be a pause as each passenger handed over their documents. The voice got closer and closer, until it was on top of us. Still we kept our eyes closed. I could feel my eyelids shaking.

'*Pass bitte? … Pass bitte?*' the guard said to us.

I prayed they would carry on through the carriage, but this guard had other ideas.

'*Wecke deinen Vater auf.*'

What did that mean? I hoped it meant 'It's okay, they're asleep' but somehow I wasn't so sure.

Then I realised. Hessam had opened his eyes. The guard was asking him to wake Dad. *'Wecke deinen Vater auf'* meant 'Wake your father up.'

I peeped through a half-open eye and saw the guard tapping Dad on the shoulder.

*'Pass bitte,'* he repeated as Dad opened his eyes. There was nothing else for it.

Dad looked up at the guard and said, 'Refugee.'

Unlike the man at passport control at the airport, the guard seemed to know exactly what Dad meant. So did all the other passengers, and we could suddenly feel the stares of the whole carriage. I always hated it when people stared. It made me want to stand up and tell them why we were there. About the execution order, Mum's bravery, Hussein's illness. About being robbed and made to eat all that pizza. But the guard was already ushering us through the carriage. It seemed we weren't welcome on this train any more.

Dad was quickly trying to think of what to do. We were expected by a new handler in the Netherlands in just a few hours, and now we had no idea where we were being taken. So much for the easy ride.

We did what we were told and got off the train. Then we watched as our ride to the Netherlands disappeared into the distance. We were at a small local station, and almost immediately we were met by the police. They asked us to sit in yet another waiting room while they fetched us some water and food. Then they asked Mum and Dad loads of questions. They weren't as kind as Lukas, but at least they weren't trying to steal from us.

Mum and Dad answered the questions the best they could. I didn't understand much, but I could tell they were giving false names again. Not James and John this time, but the surname Akbar. Hussein giggled. 'I wonder what we'll be next,' he said.

After a few more questions, the border control police took us back to the train stop. I could tell Dad was still desperately trying to think of a plan to get us back on our journey. Mum's plan was to pray. As we stood there, another train drew up. The border police gave us a handful of tickets and told us to get on. What was happening? Why were we allowed back on the train?

We looked at the tickets. They didn't say much, but we could tell the destination was somewhere back in Germany. The Belgian police explained that they'd informed the German police we were coming and we'd be handed straight back to them when we got there.

But the guards showed no sign of getting on the train with us. They simply waved us off and left it at that. I looked at Dad. He winked. I could tell he had no intention of ending up back in Germany.

'Come on,' said Dad as soon as we were back on the train. 'We're not staying on this train any longer than we have to.' We moved to seats near the door and, as soon as we reached the first stop, we all got off.

We stepped down onto the platform of another Belgian station. We didn't know where we were or how far it was to the Dutch border, but this time Dad was on a mission. He found a payphone and straight away called the handler. I could see him shouting down the phone to him.

'You were full of shit. What are we supposed to do now?' I could hear him saying.

The conversation lasted a few more minutes, and then Dad came back. Well?

'He says to get on the next train to Holland,' said Dad. 'But we're going to have to get some tickets first.' Thankfully we still had some money left from the takeaway job, and, using a combination of sign language and the word 'Holland', Dad managed to buy the tickets.

We had to wait about half an hour for the next train, but once we were on it, the rest of the journey couldn't have been easier. There didn't seem to be any guards at the border, and no one asked us for anything. No one even mentioned passports. We sailed into the Netherlands as if nothing had happened. I could almost feel Dad relaxing and, although Mum wasn't so calm, at least we knew we were one step closer.

That didn't mean there wasn't trouble ahead.

# CHAPTER 11

# The pit

We reached the Netherlands a few hours later. The train stopped and everyone got up. It seemed this was the last stop. Hussein and Hessam were asleep, but Dad gently shook them awake and we gathered our things. We stepped down onto the platform and waited as the other passengers moved off to their destinations. Eventually we were the only ones left, standing at the entrance to yet another country on our own. We scanned the area for police, but it seemed pretty quiet. Dad said we should look out for the next handler too, who should be there to meet us.

After a while Dad spotted something. Sure enough, there was a man at the other end of the station waving at us. Dad walked cautiously over to him.

The robbery had affected Mum quite a lot, and she seemed nervous as Dad spoke to the handler. But when Dad returned he said that everything was okay, it was the right handler and he'd been given a description of us by the first guy. He knew who we were and would take us to the next location. Dad also said he was keen to get going.

'We're too vulnerable out in the open,' he said. 'Plus, I'm sick of thinking up new names for my kids.'

It was a short walk to the car park and we were told to get into a hidden compartment in the boot of a car. My heart sank. We'd got used to riding in the back seat instead of being tangled together in a tiny space.

'I know it's not a private jet, boys,' smiled Dad, 'but you can't always get the VIP treatment.'

We folded ourselves into the boot as Dad got into the passenger seat. I was excited in a way – with every new country we were closer to the UK. The end was starting to feel real.

There was no bumpy ride this time. In fact, we weren't in the car for very long when we stopped and were told to get out. We unfolded ourselves from the boot, and saw that it was already dark. The handler told us to walk slowly behind his friend.

'Don't say a word,' he ordered, and I felt like I was in some sort of stakeout in a movie. We crept along in the darkness, through thick bushes and long grass. Who knew where we were, and I had a horrible feeling we were heading for another jungle, like the one in Ukraine.

As we continued along the path, the bushes suddenly opened up. I could just about make out a sort of pit between the trees. My eyes were used to the dark by now, and I could see a group of people – they looked like families – standing in the clearing. They were waiting, each standing in one corner of the pit, almost hiding. Behind the pit were some more bushes and then a lorry park, like a lay-by at the side of the road.

'What is it?' I whispered, my curiosity getting the better of me. Dad shushed me, and Mum squeezed my hand as if to say 'be quiet'.

What we saw then was a bit like a play, with everyone carrying out their different role.

After a while, one of the handlers would flag down a lorry to make it stop in the lay-by. He'd approach the driver's cab and say he needed to check documents. He'd then direct him to a parking spot near the pit area, where the handler would ask to see his licence and passport. While the driver was searching for his papers, the handler would make small talk about where the lorry was going. As soon as the driver told him his destination, the handler would give a sign to one of the families hiding in the darkness. They would then go behind the back of the lorry, where another handler would put a ladder up to the top of the lorry.

The family would climb up the ladder and onto the roof of the lorry. Up they went, onto the soft top of the vehicle, until you couldn't see them any more. Then we'd hear a quiet rip. This was them cutting a hole through the soft top of the lorry with a knife so they could climb down into the container.

We watched this happen over and over again as the handlers pulled more lorries into the lay-by. Each time a different family would disappear up onto the lorry and drop down inside it. What happened to the family after that? How long were they in that lorry? Did they ever get caught? It seemed to work like clockwork but I didn't think it could be that easy.

One thing I noticed was that the handlers didn't really seem to care where the lorries were going. In fact, I saw them tell one family their lorry was going to the UK when I'd heard the driver say he was going to Turkey. This was so unfair! How could they tell them they were going to the UK when they knew the family were going to end up thousands of miles in the wrong direction? I didn't want to think about it too much, but I also knew that people died in these lorries – I had overheard stories of customers at the takeaway, and heard the parents whisper to each other when we were in the jungle in Russia, and thought we weren't listening. I suddenly imagined being stuck in a container for days, never reaching your destination and watching your parents and siblings slowly die in front of you.

But we didn't have much choice. Neither did the other families in the pit. One by one more lorries were stopped, and the group of people got smaller and smaller. At one point one of the handlers came over to Dad. We thought it might be our turn, but instead he started shouting at him. It turned out it was about our luggage – we needed to make sure we could easily fit into a container so we needed to get rid of some of our stuff.

How could we get rid of some stuff when we only had one backpack for the five of us? Mum opened the bag to see what we could take out. I noticed she didn't touch the photos she'd stuffed in the back of the bag. I knew Mum, and there was no way she was going to leave those behind. Instead she brought out some of the spare clothes and added them to a large pile that was forming at the side of the pit. We helped her, and it was hard not to look through some of the things other people had left behind. Clothes, bags, toiletries, but also photos and jewellery. These were memories. How could people leave them behind at the side of the road?

Finally, there was only us and a couple of other families left. The sky was starting to get light, and I wondered what would happen to us if we were still here at dawn. As it got bluer and bluer overhead, Dad started to look worried. I was scared of travelling in the back of a container lorry, but I also knew that right now this was the only option we had. We didn't have a back-up. Time was running out.

Another lorry was flagged down, and as a handler spoke to the driver Dad was called over by another. The man handed him a big knife and motioned to us to go with him.

'Stay close to us,' Dad whispered, and 'Look after Mum,' he added to me.

I could feel the familiar rush of adrenaline as we went round to the back of the lorry. The sky was really light now. What if the lorry driver noticed we were climbing up a ladder onto the back of his truck?

Then the handler talking to the driver made a signal to us. That meant the destination was good, or so they said. Now we just had to wait to be told when to climb up to the top of the lorry.

I could hear Hussein's breathing getting heavier behind me. It didn't sound good. It was rasping, and I knew that meant he was struggling to control his heart rate. I had to calm him down somehow. I looked around, and suddenly spotted a beautiful black horse in the field on the other side of the pit. We always talked about having a horse one day, so I nudged Hussein and pointed to it on the other side of the bushes. It worked. I saw him focus on the horse, controlling his breathing and slowing his heart rate. That horse helped me too, as it took the focus off what we were about to do for a minute.

'I'm okay, I'm okay,' Hussein was muttering. I don't know whether he was talking to me or himself. After a few minutes I could hear his breathing return to normal.

While we were looking at the horse the handler must have given the signal to climb the ladder. Before we knew it, Dad was pushing us towards the lorry and we tripped towards the back wheels. I didn't know what to do, and was about to start climbing the ladder when the handler suddenly turned around to face us. 'Stop!' he whispered loudly.

Why did we have to stop? Confused, I waited at the ladder, my foot on the bottom rung. What was going on? Why did we have to stop? He came and grabbed onto me, holding me back from going any further. I could see Dad looking around wildly.

'No signal. No go,' the handler was saying. We'd misunderstood.

And that was it. The time was up. The window was closed and the sky was getting lighter and lighter. The handler grabbed the knife from Dad and put it away.

'Tomorrow,' he said, 'hopefully.' And with that all the handlers just wandered back into the bushes and left us, abandoning us in the middle of nowhere by a busy road.

'What are we supposed to do now?' asked Mum in despair.

'No idea,' said Dad. But the sky was light now, so the first thing we needed to do was find somewhere to hide. We were standing right out in the open and the lorries were whizzing past us. If anyone saw us we'd be arrested.

'Let's go that way,' said Hussein suddenly. He was pointing away from the pit and out of the line of sight. Mum looked concerned.

'Why that way?' she asked, but I could see why. It was the field where we'd seen the horse a few moments ago.

It seemed as good a place as any, so we all traipsed through the bushes and towards the field. As we came through the hedge we could see there was some kind of town, or at least some streets, on the other side of the field. Perhaps we could get some food. I suddenly realised I was starving, as we hadn't had a proper meal for a couple of days.

Keeping a close eye on the group of horses, Dad led us through the field. Hussein and I both loved horses. We tried to find an excuse to get closer and closer to them, but I could tell Mum just wanted us out of there.

As we got alongside the horses Dad started picking up the pace, heading for a wooden gate at the far end of the field. But as he speeded up we also started to walk quicker, and before I knew it I'd broken into a run. Hussein and Hessam followed and suddenly we were all running through the field towards the gate.

I've never been scared of horses, but being in the field with them didn't feel quite right. Seeing us start to run like that made them agitated, and they started to move towards us, getting faster. Soon they were galloping crazily through the field, and as they got closer, we ran even faster. It wasn't until we were nearly at the gate that I realised Hussein was no longer behind me. I smacked my forehead. Why had I not stayed behind him like I normally did? I looked back, and I could see him crouched on one knee in the middle of the field, rubbing his chest.

I swore. 'It's okay!' he was trying to shout, as usual trying to convince us there was nothing wrong. I could see the blood rushing to his head. 'Mum!' I shouted.

But she'd already seen what was happening. She shouted, 'Hussein!' and I saw her start to run back towards him. It was awful watching him on the floor, struggling for breath – was he going to have a blackout? They were rare, but had started to happen more frequently.

Time seemed to slow down then, but the horses didn't. They were really spooked, and started to rush towards Hussein in the middle of the field. That was when Dad took charge. He ran to Hussein and shouted at Mum to take Hessam and me out of the field. Mum looked back at Hussein but did what she was told, grabbing us and starting to pull us towards the wooden gate.

But I didn't want to leave Hussein. I'd been protecting him all my life. I wasn't about to let him die in a field of horses.

'I'm going,' I shouted, and managed to break free of Mum. Dad saw me rushing back into the field and shouted at me to go back. I think he thought I was messing around.

The horses were still rushing towards Hussein, and while Dad ran to help him, I decided to do what I knew best: cause a distraction. I waved my arms around and shouted like a maniac, hoping I could get the horses to turn their attention from Hussein to me. Dad reached Hussein and scooped him up, and I suddenly realised my plan had worked. The horses were heading straight for me.

Then it didn't seem like such a clever idea. As the horses galloped towards me I could feel my legs shaking. But I stood still, waiting, waving my arms until Dad had got Hussein over the gate.

Then I was really scared. As soon as Hussein was clear I bolted, running faster than I'd ever run before away from the charging horses. I could see Mum at the gate, her arms open and ready for me. I reached the gate just as I felt the vibrations of the horses' hooves behind me.

I quickly realised there was no time to climb over, but I remembered something I'd seen on a TV show back in Moscow, where the hero flings himself through the gap in a gate. So I fixed my sight on the gap between the wooden bars and hoped for the best. It couldn't be that hard, could it?

As I got to the gate I knew I just had to go for it, so I screwed up my eyes and threw myself into the gap. Dad shouted an incoherent sound. I landed on something soft.

When I opened my eyes I could see the stubble on Dad's chin. I'd jumped straight into his arms and was now pressed up against his face as we lay on the grass. We were both breathing heavily but managed to stand up. The horses had run right up to the gate and were looking at us wildly.

Mum cried and hugged me tightly as I untangled myself from Dad. 'I'm alright,' I said. 'I think.' Hussein, who was slowly managing to get his breath back, stood up from the ground too. As soon as he could talk he reached over and flicked me on the head.

'Nutter,' he said.

CHAPTER 12

# lorry cargo

Now that we were safely through the field, we had to find somewhere to wait until nightfall. We also really needed some food.

We headed for what looked like the small town and found a local corner shop. Dad bought as much as he could carry in his arms and we ate it sitting by the pavement.

Now we just had to keep a low profile until it went dark. If any police saw us they could ask us for our documents and we'd be in trouble.

We wandered around, feeling exhausted. Hussein's episode in the field made us realise how much worse he'd become and how little time we had left to get him to a proper hospital. The longer we spent out in the open with no shelter and not enough sleep or food, the worse he would surely feel. I noticed that he was much less talkative these days, and I knew that meant he was tired from the extra effort his heart was having to make to keep him going.

Hussein never let on that he was struggling, and he kept the spikes in his heart rate mostly to himself. But I would see it sometimes – a change in the colour of his face or a short-ness in his breathing. He tried to cover it up but I could tell that he felt like his heart was popping out of his chest.

We decided it wasn't a good idea to stay near the shops as they were too out in the open. Dad said we didn't look like other people in the town. I asked if it was because we were Afghan. 'No,' he said, 'it's because you and Hussein are covered in mud.'

So we headed back towards the fields. We definitely didn't want to go near any horses, so we aimed for a bushy area that was away from houses and shops.

As we traipsed back through the undergrowth, Mum prayed. I just wished it would get dark, which was funny, because Hussein and I spent most of our lives *not* wanting it to get dark. Back in Herat we'd be out playing football in the alleyway, hoping the evening would stretch a few more hours until curfew.

Eventually we came to a bare patch in the undergrowth and Mum found a muddy log we could sit on. We spent a few hours there, bored out of our minds and impatient for the next part of our journey.

We huddled in a circle like we used to around the *sofra*. Suddenly I began to laugh. 'Did you see me dive through that gate?'

Hussein caught the giggles too. 'You should have seen the look on your face with those horses running up your ass,' he said. Mum rolled her eyes, and we all joined in. Dad ruffled my hair. Whatever happened, I knew we'd always have this.

We spent the rest of the afternoon teasing and joking with each other and jumping on and off the log, but we were glad to see the light fading in the sky. Dad kept his eyes peeled for police patrols, and he also told us to watch out for any sign of the handlers who'd ditched us the night before. As night started to fall he seemed anxious to get back to the pit. We had to make sure we were first in line this time.

Suddenly Dad whispered, 'Shhh.' We could hear people nearby.

'Get behind Mum – by that tree,' Dad said, pointing to a big tree a few feet away. We didn't know if the rustling was the handlers or local police, so it was best to be on the safe side.

From behind the tree I could see Dad stepping carefully towards the noise, looking around him for something to use in self-defence. After our journey so far, I didn't blame him.

Mum gripped onto us tighter as we peeked out from behind the branches, and I saw Dad pick up a log.

But Dad soon realised a log would be no use. We heard a voice say, 'Drop that,' and suddenly a group of men came out of the bushes. Some of them had machetes. Outnumbered and out-armed, Dad had no choice but to drop his weapon to the floor.

'Who are you and what are you doing?' asked one of them firmly. He seemed a bit cross. I held my breath as Mum came out from behind the tree.

'Please, don't hurt us,' she said.

'We were left behind last night,' Dad explained quickly, realising these must be traffickers. The men looked at one another. I looked at their faces to see if I could recognise any of them, and to see if any of them would recognise us.

There was a long pause, and I could see Dad frantically thinking of a way out, probably by offering the little money we had left. Hussein held on to Hessam and me tightly, as if stopping us from making a move that could make the men even angrier.

'Wait,' came a voice suddenly from the back of the group. Dad tried to see where it was coming from, when rustling through the bushes came another man. He stopped, looked at all of us, whispered into one of the machete men's ears and then disappeared back into the trees.

Dad looked desperate. He started to put his hand in his pocket to count how much money he had left to bribe the traffickers with. It wasn't a lot.

One of the men waved his hand. 'It's okay,' he said. 'Stop.'

Dad looked confused. Did that mean they recognised us from the night before?

'It's okay,' he repeated, and brought his machete down. He called us over. Slowly, we came out of the bushes and headed towards Dad. They remembered who we were. The traffickers motioned us to the pit, and once again we arrived at the lay-by at the side of the road.

We weren't the first there. We could see several other families already waiting. Not wanting to take any chances, Dad headed over to what looked like the main trafficker and started to speak to him. He was determined not to spend another night in this pit.

When Dad came back to us, we settled into our groups and waited where the traffickers showed us. Before long the lorries started to stop. It was just like the night before, but this time we weren't so scared about climbing onto that lorry. We just wanted to get away.

As we waited in the pit, Hussein and I played the fool together. Most of the time we acted like normal brothers. But we weren't normal brothers – we were about to cut our way into a truck.

While we played, Dad and Mum seemed stressed, and the men got on with their work putting traffic cones at the side of the road. A few hovered towards the back of the pit with the knives and ladder. We waited.

The sky was totally dark now, and all the families were in groups in different parts of the pit.

We hoped and prayed that we'd be the first to go. We'd been waiting since last night, and were one of the first families here. Dad paced around, making sure the traffickers didn't forget he was there.

Suddenly came a 'Shhhh' from one of them, and Dad stopped pacing. Was it us? Was it our turn now?

'You,' said the man, pointing to the group right next to us. Dad sighed. Why not us? It wasn't fair.

The chosen family were taken to the edge of the lay-by, given the knife and the ladder was leaned against the lorry. All this only took a few minutes, giving us hope that things would move quickly tonight. Perhaps we'd be next.

Not long after, another sign was given – to another group. Dad sighed again. Maybe third time lucky, I thought.

In the darkness I could see another lorry being stopped and, after speaking with the driver, the trafficker gave another sign.

Then: 'It's time,' he said to Dad. I couldn't believe it. I felt a rush of adrenaline as Dad quickly grabbed us and pushed us towards the edge of the pit. We were handed the knife and waited patiently for the signal to go. Dad was given a final run-through of what we had to do and we were shuffled into the right order for climbing the ladder. Then he received a nod.

'Go, go,' a trafficker whispered, as he pushed Dad towards the ladder.

'Hold on to me,' Dad said to us all, and we hurried up behind him. The timing had to be just right, and we knew from watching the other families that every second counted.

Dad climbed quickly up the ladder, then Hussein, Hessam, Mum and me.

After a couple of seconds I could see that Dad had already reached the roof of the lorry. He took a quick glance behind him to see that we were all up too and then before we knew it he was attacking the lining of the roof with the knife. All he had to do was make a hole big enough for us to fit through.

He cut four corners first, just like the trafficker had told him, to make a big square. At this point I heard something behind me and noticed that the ladder was being taken away. Why were they doing that? What if we couldn't get in? It seemed we were on our own now, and had no choice but to get inside it before the driver drove off.

With all four corners cut, I saw Dad jump down inside the vehicle. It was dark inside, and I couldn't see where he landed. But I saw his face as he looked up at us and motioned for us to follow him one by one.

Suddenly there was a rush of noise and the lorry started to vibrate. It was moving off! I felt the driver put it into gear, and I knew that in a matter of seconds we'd be on the road. Mum had helped Hessam and Hussein through the hole and was climbing in herself, with Dad underneath still trying to make room. But I was still on top of the lorry. Suddenly I felt like I was moving backwards. Terrified, I realised this was because the lorry was moving forward, and I was being thrown backwards onto the canopy. There was no ladder and nothing to hold on to. Was I about to fall off a moving truck?

I clung desperately onto the tarpaulin covering the lorry, but in less than a second I felt Dad's strong arm grab me. He must have reached up through the roof and taken hold of my shirt. Mum was in, and just as the lorry started to move Dad dragged me in through the hole into the darkness. I fell with a thud just as we started to pick up speed.

Falling into a moving lorry was one thing, but not knowing what I was falling into was another. I landed head-first into something rubbery, and soon realised I was stuck in a stack of tyres. I kicked my legs, trying to turn around and get out of my trap, but I was stuck. To make things worse, I could hear Hussein and Hessam laughing behind me.

'Help!' I whispered, just in case the lorry driver could hear us. The blood was rushing to my head. Hussein was sniggering. It was kind of funny, but I still really needed to get myself the right way up so I could get out of those tyres.

Dad started to whisper instructions to me, showing me how to turn myself around in the tiny space, and soon I managed to stand upright again.

We looked around the inside of the lorry. It was still dark outside, and we could see the stars through the gap Dad had cut in the roof. At least we were inside the truck. At one point I thought I'd be squashed like roadkill on the tarmac outside. But where were we going? We only had the traffickers' word for it that we were going in the right direction. They said we were heading for Calais and then across the channel to the UK, but we all knew there was a chance we could be heading back the way we'd come. The thought that we might be taking Hussein further away from the help he needed instead of towards it made my tummy feel empty.

All we could do was stay put and hope. We spent the first hour or two reliving the last two days, talking over all the things that had happened in the pit. But after a while we felt the lorry start to slow down. Were we stopping? Mum told us to hide among the tyres just in case. It was probably a pit stop for the driver she said. She didn't think anyone would open the back.

As the lorry came to a stop I could hear noises outside. People were talking, and I could hear car engines. We must have been underneath a street light or something, as there was a bright light shining through the gap in the roof. It was like a spotlight, and it started to hurt my eyes.

I found a space among the tyres and crept in, making as little noise as I could. I pulled my legs up so no one could see me and tried hard to listen to what was going on outside. I could just about see Dad opposite me and, although I couldn't see the others, it was so quiet in the truck that I could just about hear them breathing.

We heard the driver get out, and there was a sudden change in the light above us. It seemed to get even brighter, shining down into the lorry on top of us. We could still hear talking, and I could just about make out the heavy steps of the driver. It sounded like he was walking towards the container doors. Everyone stayed quiet, and Dad motioned to me to stay still.

Mum had said they probably wouldn't open the back, but suddenly there was a loud clunk of locks and rotating hinges. It sounded like they were opening the back to me! Sure enough, the container doors opened with a huge creaking noise. The rust between the hinges made the metal look orange.

I didn't move. I could see Dad's face opposite me but I sat like a statue, holding my breath so I didn't make any noise at all. All we could do was stay still and hope they didn't spot us. I could hear the driver having a pretty serious conversation with someone, and from their voices I thought they must be border control police.

Suddenly, a torch light shone through the tyres and scanned the inside of the lorry. Surely it wouldn't be able to pick us out hiding inside the tyres? I'd be okay as long as I didn't make a noise.

The search went on for ages. Then the border police seemed to tell the driver to close the huge container doors, and we heard the hinges lock together. There was a final clunk of the lock by the driver and all was quiet again.

I heard everyone let out a big rush of air, and I realised I wasn't the only one who'd been holding my breath. Then I heard the driver walk around the back of the lorry and swing himself up into his seat. We were safe.

Then the engine started, and I was relieved to feel the lorry moving forward again. But as we moved, I noticed that the light above us was even brighter now. It was shining right down through the hole in the top of the lorry like a bright searchlight. Once again I could hear steps, but this time it was hard to follow them or work out where they were coming from. It was weird, but it almost sounded like they were coming from the roof.

Suddenly I looked up, and straight away I could see where the steps were coming from. Right above me, alongside the top of the lorry, I could see border police walking along a ridge. They were checking the vehicle from above.

I could see a roof through the hole in the lorry, and I realised we were at a huge metal checkpoint. The light that was coming in was from searchlights pointing down on the lorry containers. There were border police all around us. This was where they checked the lorries for refugees.

What were we going to do? The police might not have noticed us from the back of the lorry, but they'd definitely notice the huge, gaping hole in the top. Dad put his fingers to his lips and whispered, 'Shh,' to me, and I tried to tuck myself even further in to my spot inside the tyres. All we could was hope the border police wouldn't see us.

Because I was the last person to get into the lorry, I was the closest to the hole in the roof. If they looked in, I would be the person they'd see first. I held my breath again, wriggling my arms and legs to disappear further into my hole. I watched as the light from the torch above changed direction. Suddenly the steps of the border police were quicker. My heart was beating out of my chest.

Then: '*Nous avons quelque chose,*' I heard the police guard say. He shouted to one of his workmates, and I heard someone else shouting in the distance. The driver turned the engine off.

I looked straight at Dad, panic rising in my chest. He was looking straight back at me, and I could tell by his face that there was nothing I could do. I just had to stay quiet. Suddenly I felt the light of a torch shining on me and I looked up. Above me, looking down into the hole, was a border guard, and he was shining his light straight into my face.

'Dad …' I whispered slowly.

But Dad didn't say anything. He just put his fingers to his lips again and shook his head. He couldn't see the border guard above me and if I moved I would definitely be found out. How could I let him know I was staring straight up at the police?

'Dad …' I tried again.

He widened his eyes at me crossly and mouthed, 'Hush.' But I knew the game was up.

I wriggled my hand free from the tyres and pointed straight up. 'He can see me,' I said.

Dad quickly looked up. He could see straight away there was no getting away from this one.

The border guards above us were babbling away in French now and shining their torches, obviously trying to see how many others were hiding in the lorry. They were shouting at the lorry driver and he was shouting back. He was obviously in big trouble and I almost felt sorry for him. How was he supposed to know he had a family of five as cargo?

'Come out, Hamed,' said Dad now, and I started to unfold myself out of the tyres. One by one the others came out too. What was going to happen to us now? We were in big trouble, that was for sure, and we'd just have to do as we were told. There was definitely no way to make a run for it.

More police came, and someone eventually dropped a ladder down into the container so we could climb out. Feeling like criminals, we started to climb up the ladder and out into the light.

As we came out of the lorry we knew we must be at the French border. There were French police everywhere, and lorries were queuing to be searched. We were so close to the UK we could almost feel it. We got out of the lorry and watched as it disappeared into the distance. I wondered whether the driver would have to go to prison and I wanted to tell them it wasn't his fault.

We hung around on some metal ramps by the side of the search area, waiting to be taken to the processing room. We knew the routine: us boys would (hopefully) be given some food while the police asked Mum and Dad loads of questions.

Sure enough, after a few minutes the guards brought us something to eat and then started to grill Dad. I could hear him giving them yet more false names and I supposed it was so they couldn't trace us back to another location. The last thing we wanted was to be sent back the other way.

The questions didn't take too long this time, and I guessed they could see that we were all tired. Or maybe they just didn't want us to be their problem any more. Soon after, a van arrived for us and the guards told us we were going to be taken to the camp at Calais. This was exactly what I'd been afraid of. Before we'd left Herat I'd heard lots of stories about this camp – and they weren't good.

We got into the van. It was so frustrating, knowing we were being taken in the opposite direction to where we wanted to go! At least we got to sit up front. There was no need to hide in the boot any more. We were caught, busted, found out. Dad said not to worry and to look on the bright side: we'd soon find another way. In the meantime we just had to do what we were told. But I was sick of doing what we were told. Back in Herat it was the Taliban, now it was the border police. When were we going to live somewhere we could do what we liked?

# CHAPTER 13

# Calais

O f all the places we could have ended up, the one we didn't want to visit was the Calais camp. Along our journey so far we had heard the stories of what had happened to some of the people who tried to leave that place – some of them true, others probably not – and although it was close to the UK, we'd become terrified of the thought of it. Dad said it would be okay and we'd be out of here in no time. Mum didn't look so confident.

I tried to look on the bright side and tell myself the camp probably wasn't as bad as everyone made out. I tried not to be scared.

When we got to the outskirts of the camp we had to go through registration. Dad gave them our new false names again, and Mum told us not to speak in case we accidentally got mixed up about who we were and where we'd come from.

Then we stayed with Mum in a waiting area while Dad went off to find our room. Hussein was tired, so he and Hessam lay down across the seats while Mum and I went to find the canteen.

After we'd had some food, we went straight to our new accommodation. It didn't feel as friendly and welcoming as in Austria. Our room was dirty and you could hear noises coming from other places around the camp from inside it. Dad said we should go straight to bed as the journey had been long and tiring. As I lay under the scratchy sheets I could hear Mum and Dad discussing things in whispers. Mum said she was worried about what was going to happen, but Dad reassured her, saying we should remember other families who weren't so lucky.

'What about Hussein?' she said. 'We're putting him through too much.'

'It's okay, he's strong,' replied Dad. 'He's never been able to do what the other boys can, but does he ever complain? He's a special boy, Fariba. If anyone's going to beat the odds and survive this thing it'll be him.'

'I'm worried about Hamed and Hessam too,' said Mum. 'They have to take the burden of Hussein on themselves.'

'I know,' whispered Dad. 'But they understand more than you think. Have you seen how they look after him? How they adjust what they do to make sure he can keep up? They're a team.'

There was silence.

'I just want to be able to tell them we've made it,' said Mum.

I must have fallen asleep then, as the next thing I knew I was waking up in the bed I was sharing with my brothers.

I could hear seagulls, and I remembered that we were near the sea. Dad was already up and seemed to be in a good mood after some sleep. He was humming a tune, and I could tell he was on a mission to get us out of here and across to the UK. He was busy making calls, probably trying to find a handler who could get us on the next stage of our journey. I never knew how he did this, but each time he did it seemed like magic.

Hussein was still asleep, so I sat by Dad as he made his phone calls. He haggled over the phone, trying to negotiate the best deal to get us out of here. 'No,' he'd say, 'that was too unsafe …' 'No – too expensive …' 'No, that's a risk we're not prepared to take.' I didn't know there were so many options. The way Dad was talking reminded me of the Moscow market – everyone arguing over what price they would pay. But this wasn't haggling for bread or cheese. It was haggling over us.

Dad was on the phone for ages, but eventually he seemed to be getting somewhere. He was still talking about group discounts and per person rates. How could these people treat us like this? Didn't they understand Hussein was ill? We weren't objects to be squeezed in or forced across the border. Then Dad seemed to be getting annoyed with the conversation, and he put the phone down and sighed.

'Is it no good?' I asked.

'Not yet.' Dad managed a smile.

Suddenly we heard someone knocking at the door. I couldn't think who it could be, as we didn't know anyone here. Nervously, Dad opened the door, but when he saw who was on the other side he immediately laughed out loud and grabbed the person in a huge hug.

'That's a friendly face!' he was laughing. Clapping this stranger on the back, Dad hurried him into the room. I had no idea who this was, so was a bit surprised when he grabbed my cheeks and said, 'This must be one of your boys.'

Dad introduced us. 'This is Ali Reza,' he said. 'He's a friend of your uncle's. He left Herat a few months before us.'

Then Dad and Ali Reza talked and talked about boring things, but because the others were still asleep I stayed to listen. My ears pricked up when Dad asked Ali Reza how long he'd been here in the camp.

'Thirty days,' he said. 'And counting. We've had a few attempts to get out, but no luck so far.'

'How many times?' asked Dad.

'Oh, just a few!' laughed Ali Reza. 'Maybe fourteen?'

Dad's face fell and his eyes widened. So did mine. How could so many attempts have failed? I wondered where this guy was going wrong. Was it really that hard to get out of here and across to the UK? What if we were here for a month like him? What if we never left? I knew from what had happened in the field in the Netherlands that we didn't have that long. Hussein would need his treatment before then.

Then Dad and Ali Reza started to talk about the best ways to get across. Dad said he'd had no luck trying to arrange something with the handlers as it was all too risky or expensive. We didn't know anyone or have any real contacts. It seemed impossible.

Ali Reza started to tell Dad about some of the attempts he'd made. One of them had been by raft, and when it had sunk there weren't enough lifejackets for everyone. The raft had been overcrowded, with too many people on it in the first place, and everyone ended up in the water. The traffickers were so terrified of being spotted that they told everyone to swim under water, even holding people's heads under so they wouldn't be discovered. Not everyone made it back to the camp alive.

Dad's eyes darted at me and Ali Reza took the hint. I felt a rush of fear. Surely Dad wasn't going to put us and Mum through something like that? Or did he think that sort of thing was worth a try?

They started to talk about other options, and it came up that Ali Reza had a chance to leave that evening. Dad was interested.

We shouldn't get too hopeful, Ali Reza told us – there might not be any spaces left. And even if there were, it might not work at all. But I could tell Dad was going to get us on that trip if he could. After all, he'd promised us he'd get us out of here.

'What do we need to do?' he said.

They started to discuss the details, but Ali Reza didn't seem to really know what the trip would involve. After a bit more discussion he was off, saying he'd see if he could arrange five spaces for us. Dad seemed excited. 'Let's go and tell the others,' he said.

I felt a bit scared, although Dad did promise the attempt wouldn't be on a raft. Before we got to the others, he took me to one side and made me make a promise: 'Don't tell the others about the fourteen other attempts.'

I nodded and Dad said, 'That's my boy.'

*

The others were awake now, and Dad explained to them what the escape would involve. He said it wouldn't be without danger, but he'd known Ali Reza for years and could vouch for his reliability. Besides, we had to try.

Hussein suddenly stood up. 'Let's do this,' he said. He was the one who found everything the most difficult, and yet he was always the first person willing to try.

Dad had another warning. 'We also mustn't get our hopes up,' he said. 'There might not even be any spaces for us tonight. Ali Reza is doing all he can and is hoping to pull some strings, but we mustn't be too disappointed if he can't.'

We waited impatiently for night time. Dad was distracted, and I could tell he was trying to think of a back-up plan in case this didn't work. Finally, Ali Reza burst through the door with good news.

The handler arranging the attempt was willing to take us tonight – as long as we paid some 'tax' for the short notice and extra luggage. It took me a minute to realise that 'luggage' meant us. Dad didn't argue and immediately gave Ali Reza the fee and told us to get ready.

The next few hours went by slowly. We played around a bit to pass the time, but we all got quieter and quieter as the hour for leaving got nearer. I knew by now that these journeys were unpredictable, and that each one seemed to get harder for Hussein. The story of the raft was still going round in my mind.

Eventually it was time to go. Leaving the camp at night was easier than we thought. It was as if the camp controllers knew everyone there was trying to get out, and they didn't even try to stop us. We just walked to the arranged meeting point, Dad holding Hessam's hand and Mum holding mine and Hussein's. Before long we saw Ali Reza waving at us from a group of about ten people, and we knew that these were the people we were going to spend the journey with.

One of the men in the group was pacing around and looking at his watch, and I guessed this must be the handler. He looked stressed and kept looking at the camp exits. Before long he called us all over. He wasn't Afghan, but he spoke to us in Farsi.

'You're going to have to do a *lot* of walking, so be prepared,' he said. Everyone in the group nodded in agreement. Except us. We all looked at Hussein. Would he be able to keep up? I saw Mum squeeze his hand.

'We'll be okay,' she said. 'We'll stick together and (*inshallah*) get there safely.' She looked at Hussein and then at us. 'Whatever happens, we don't split up, okay?' She paused. 'Hussein? Can you do this?' She was giving him a chance to pull out, to cancel the whole thing and no one would be cross. But we all knew how Hussein would respond to that.

'Let's do this,' he smiled. It was becoming his catchphrase.

With no time to waste the handler started to make his way towards a tarmac path that led out of the camp. We all followed slowly behind. It was pitch black and I could hardly even see my feet in front of me. I wished we had a torch. No one could see where they were going or what they might be stepping in; I could only follow Dad's breathing and the sound of his footsteps. Hussein followed behind me, and I

heard him breathe in and out, slowly and deeply in the darkness. This was what he did to steady his breathing. I hoped
he'd be okay.

Everyone was very quiet as we made our way through
the darkness. Who knew where we were going? Mum was
right behind Hussein, so I knew she would spot if anything
went wrong or he was struggling. We just had to trust that
we'd be okay. Mum kept whispering little things to us to take
our minds off all the walking – things like 'You know you'll
always be my babies. Even when you're older and you get
married, you'll still be babies to me.' Hussein and I giggled.
Typical Mum. But at least it passed the time.

After we'd walked for what felt like hours, something
suddenly broke the blackness ahead of us. It was a flashing
blue light. Police? This was bad. The one thing we'd learnt
over the last few months of travelling around was that the
police were not usually on our side.

Dad and a few others in the group quickly looked around
for somewhere to hide, but then the handler did something
really strange. He told us to carry on walking.

'Just stay on the path,' he called to us. I wondered whether
we could actually trust this guy, and whether or not Ali Reza
was trying to help us after all. The blue lights were getting
closer and closer now, and Dad asked the handler whether
he was sure we shouldn't hide. But the handler just said, 'No.
Don't worry. Trust me.'

I'd heard that before, and it normally meant that we
couldn't. But what choice did we have, in the middle of the
night in the pitch black? We had to keep walking. The blue
lights were even nearer now, and there wasn't time to find

somewhere to hide anyway. We'd just have to trust what the handler said.

As the lights got closer we could see that they did in fact belong to a police van, and once it was alongside us it pulled up and stopped next to the group. Even in the darkness I could tell that Dad was angry that the handler could be so stupid. 'I told you so!' he whispered angrily. 'Caught, before we've even got going.'

The police officer rolled down the window of the van and shone his torch over the group.

'*S'il vous plaît, restez hors de la rue,*' he said. Then he rolled up his window and drove off.

We were confused. Why hadn't he arrested us? What did he say?

'Just keep going,' the handler said, and carried on walking.

Dad caught up with him. 'What just happened?' he asked.

'Those police don't care about where we're going,' the handler said to Dad. 'They just don't want us to get hit. He told us to stay off the road.' He shrugged.

'Is that it? They don't care?' asked Dad. This was new – police who didn't care about refugees escaping across the border? But sure enough, the blue light was disappearing into the distance and we were still walking. The handler was right.

We walked a bit further, and after a while I could tell that Hessam's legs were getting tired. There was still no light in sight and we had no idea how much further we'd have to walk. He was getting slower, and every now and then he'd trip over his own feet. Eventually he turned back to Dad and said, 'I think you need to do a piggyback.'

I heard Dad say, 'Okay,' and I could just make out him leaning forward in the darkness to swing Hessam up onto his back. But Hessam pulled away.

'No, not me,' he said, and pointed behind us. 'Hussein.'

Dad laughed in the darkness. 'Okay, little one, if you say so,' he said, and without another word he swapped places with me and pulled Hussein up onto his shoulders. Dad must be getting stronger, I thought. It was normally really hard for him to lift Hussein onto his shoulders. But then I realised that it was Hussein who was getting lighter.

With all our reshuffling for the piggyback, the handler was getting impatient. He called to us to keep walking and we set off again in the darkness.

Hessam was right – Hussein had needed a piggyback. I could hear him now, puffing a bit on Dad's shoulders, trying to get enough air into his lungs. At least he'd get a rest for a bit.

As we walked, we could sense that the handler was getting agitated. 'We need to get off the road!' he said suddenly. He'd stopped by a grassy field, and one by one the group caught up. There was still nothing in sight except the pitch black darkness, and I wondered why we suddenly had to change direction. He motioned to us all to get to one side, then started to direct us towards the grassy slopes at the side of the road. The grass was long, and Mum held on to us tightly as we started to walk.

As we walked further away from the road the grass got even longer, and soon it was as tall as me. It tickled my legs, arms and face, and now even the tallest children in the group were hidden from sight. I started to panic. I didn't like not being able to see the rest of my family, and all I could hear was the swish, swish of the grass around me. I could feel the grip of Mum's hand in mine, but I was scared I'd lose hold of her and be lost in the grass forever.

'Stop,' shouted the handler suddenly.

We all stopped and the shuffling went quiet. I heard Dad whisper, 'Hamed, Hessam, keep holding on tight to Mum's hand.' I could tell by the direction of his voice that he was quite far away with Hussein. No one could see where anyone was. I held on to Mum's hand as tight as I could and we followed each other through the grass as we started walking again. The group was like a big snake now, each person holding hands with the person behind them so no one would get lost. We didn't know these people – we were total strangers – but it didn't matter. The main thing was that no one lost their way in this maze of grass and that we all got out of it to safety. It reminded me of when we had to walk through the jungle with the other families in Ukraine. We all felt like we were in the same boat.

The field seemed like it went on forever, but the handler seemed to know the route. I wondered how many times he'd led people through this field. Did he do this every night?

Eventually, the handler got something out of his pocket and I realised it was a torch. Why hadn't he used the torch before? Maybe it was safer now we were in the grass. He turned it on and we followed its light, which made the walking a little bit easier at least.

After we'd walked for a few more minutes through the grass the handler stopped and waited for us all to catch up. 'We're getting close,' he said. 'Whatever happens now, you must do what I say. If you don't it will ruin it for everyone.' We all nodded. I wondered what choice we had but to do what he said in the middle of a field of tall grass in the middle of the night anyway. But again he repeated himself: 'Just do as I say, okay?'

We'd managed to catch up with Dad and Hussein by now and Dad gathered us together and held on to us tightly. 'We'll be okay, just stick together and be as quiet as possible,' he said. 'And do as he says.' Then he gave a quick hug to Hessam, who was the most frightened of the dark, and we set off behind the handler again.

'It's time. Let's go,' the handler said, and he started to walk faster than he had before. He seemed nervous now, and I wondered what was coming next. Whatever it was, it sounded dangerous, and I just wanted to get out of this field right now.

After about a minute the handler stopped and switched off his torch. Then he whispered to us all, 'Sit.' We sat down straight away, exactly where we were stood, and I could feel my heart start to beat faster, heavier. The grass was now so tall it towered over us as we sat. Hussein was still on Dad's shoulders, but even then it came to his eyes. I was worried that someone would spot him.

We sat in silence for a few minutes in the pitch black, listening to each other breathing heavily. Nothing happened except a breeze rippled through the field. I was scared. Then suddenly Hussein whispered, 'I can see a light.'

'Shh,' whispered Dad, but we could see it too. It wasn't coming from our group – it was from further away, on the other side of the field. Then suddenly there was another one. Torches. Dad looked at the handler to see how he was reacting. Then Hussein nudged him again. He pointed, and we all raised ourselves up just enough to see that there were lots of lights now, coming from every corner of the field. We were surrounded by torches.

The handler motioned to us all to lie down. So we lay in the grass, pressing our bodies as flat as we could. Dad took Hussein off his shoulders and he lay down flat in the grass, too. My heart was pounding, and I thought about Hussein's. How could he survive something as scary as this? Then came a horrible noise.

Across the field, over in the opposite corner and away from the torches, people were screaming. What was going on? People in our group began to panic, making scared noises, and the handler started shushing us, desperately.

Then there was more screaming, this time from the other side of the field. 'Other families,' whispered Mum. 'Just like us.' She looked horrified, and I suddenly felt the panic rising in my chest. They were trying to get across the border in the middle of the night, just like us. But they hadn't made it. The torches had found them.

The traffic police hadn't cared where we were going, but these border police obviously did. It was their job to catch as many refugees breaking the law as they could each night, and they didn't care how they did it. So here they were, chasing men, women, children, through a field in the middle of the night. Their search lights were closer to us now, and more and more families were getting caught. I thought this must be what a horror film was like.

'Duck, stay down!' the handler was saying in a loud whisper. 'Go deep into the grass.' We lay as flat as we could, nestling into the grass so the search lights wouldn't pick us up. I could hear the noise of the French police now, shouting to each other at the other end of the field.

Then the police seemed to move nearer. Now the search lights were right on top of us, sweeping from side to side right over where we lay in the grass. We tried to stay as still as dead bodies, waiting for them to pass. Mum and Dad held on to us to keep us from moving, but it felt like the police were closing in.

That was when it all went wrong. The tension was too much for some of the people in the group; they couldn't take it any more and started to panic. One of the men was so frightened that he started to get up. Was he going to give himself up? I stayed lying down, deep in the grass, burying my face so I couldn't see the sweep of the search lights.

Then suddenly the man who had stood up broke from the group and started to run. The lights swept round immediately and picked him up, and there were more shouts from the police. They were chasing him now and he was screaming, the light shining right on him as he ran through the grass. Where did he think he was going to run to? He was going to give us all away!

Once one of the group had run, it was like the fear spread further into the group. Others started to panic, too, and try to get away. One by one they stood up and ran, and each time the search lights would seek them out and the police would chase them down. It was just us and the handler now, lying face down in the grass. I sensed Dad gripping onto his friend. Was he panicking too?

'Let me go,' Ali Reza was whispering to Dad, almost crying with fear. 'We're just sitting ducks.' But Dad still held on
to him, pulling him back to the ground.

I was mad. These scaredy cats were going to show the
police exactly where we were. All they had to do was listen
to the handler and do as he said. Why couldn't they just do
that? By running away they were sure to get caught. At least
by staying quiet and hidden there was a chance the police
wouldn't notice us.

We lay in the grass for what felt like ages, and thought
the police lights were never going to stop. But eventually the
lights went out, and once again we were lying in complete
darkness. There was no noise from the police now. Had they
gone? For quite a while no one dared to move, but eventually
the handler looked up and nodded. 'They've gone,' he said.
Part of me couldn't believe it – I was sure we'd get caught
and arrested. Dad loosened his grip on Ali Reza's shoulder
now and we pulled ourselves up.

Mum hugged us tightly and said how brave we'd been.
We were the only ones who hadn't been caught. Then the
handler told us to start walking, so once again we followed
him through the grass, marching towards the other side of
the field. I was so terrified that the police were still here
somewhere, and I looked around me into the darkness with
every step.

But our game of hide-and-seek seemed to be over. The
grass got shorter and thinner and we could just about make
out the other side of the field, at the bottom of a hill, and
some lights in the distance. There were overhead power lines,
and I suddenly realised we were near train tracks.

Ali Reza seemed a bit calmer. I didn't say it out loud, but I thought he should be grateful. Without Dad keeping him down this would have been his fifteenth failed attempt and he'd be back in that camp.

We were at the edge of the field now and alongside the train tracks. There was a fence between us and the tracks, and the handler guided us along it. He was looking all the time at the wire mesh. I realised he was looking for a way through, a gap to get to the other side. I could see the metal of the track on the other side of the fence. Were we going to have to walk along it?

When we found the hole in the fence I realised that it had been made exactly for this purpose. It had obviously been cut with wire cutters and was just big enough for a man to climb through. Our handler had been here before. He turned to us and said, 'It's about timing now,' and I wondered what he meant. There wasn't a train in sight. It was still the middle of the night, and everywhere was dead quiet.

We climbed through the hole one by one and started to walk along the track. Dad was talking to Ali Reza, asking him some questions. Did he know what was coming next? What was the handler not telling us? Mum held on to us tightly and made sure Hessam didn't trip over the tracks. He was obviously really tired by now, and the drama in the field had terrified him. Hussein and I tried to be brave.

I was fascinated by the railway tracks, as I'd never seen them this closely before. I walked at the back of the group, wondering how we were ever going to get onto a train. Before I knew it I'd fallen behind a bit, and suddenly I heard a rustling sound. I looked up. It was coming from the other side of the fence but behind me in the field. I looked back, and before I could move or hide I suddenly saw a big dog, coming towards me. It looked like a Rottweiler and its nose was on the ground, sniffing for something. Or someone. Being pulled behind it was a uniformed police officer.

Time seemed to stop. The dog was near me now, and if I looked back I could see the dribble coming from its mouth. It could smell me, and I felt sure that if it found me it would probably eat me. I knew that our only hope of escaping the dog was by staying on this side of the fence and somehow finding somewhere to hide. I needed to catch up with the others and warn them.

But then there was another noise – a rumbling – and the track started to vibrate underneath me. I couldn't hear the group ahead of me now and I guessed the police officer wouldn't be able to either. But the dog could still smell us.

The rumble of the train got louder and louder. I needed to warn everyone, but at the same time I could feel the police dog right behind me. If I shouted to the others the police-man would hear and we'd be straight back to the camp. What could I do?

Even as I started to run I knew how it would end. I headed towards the others, hoping to warn them of the train and the dog. But running seemed to set the dog off, and straight away it started to bark.

'*Arrêtez!* STOP!' shouted the police officer, shining his torch towards me. I ran towards Mum, tears in my eyes. She turned around just as I got to her. 'I'm sorry, I'm sorry,' I called. Mum scooped me up. There was no point trying to hide now. The police officer could see us. There was nothing we could do.

The dog growled and I turned to Dad. He looked so disappointed. The police officer shone his light on us and shouted at us to stay there while he looked for a way through the fence. He talked quickly into his radio. I guessed he was telling his fellow police officers the good news.

I looked at Ali Reza, and could see his disappointment too. I felt terrible. All that walking, being hunted in that field like animals, and all for nothing. His fifteenth failed attempt. To make things worse, the train coming up behind us had now started to slow down, and I realised that this was the sign the handler had been waiting for. We were supposed to get on the train and be on our way to the UK. Seconds earlier and we'd have made it.

'I'm sorry,' I wailed at Mum again, and she hugged me tightly. Hussein came up next to me too, and I thought he was going to start teasing me for messing things up. But he just put his hand on my back and said, 'Don't worry, bro. There's always next time.' I sobbed then, knowing that every time we failed at this he got weaker and weaker. We didn't have lots of chances.

We all felt pretty depressed as we waited on the tarmac for the police van to arrive. Yes, there would be other nights and other attempts, but I wondered how much more money and effort it would take. Hussein couldn't take much more, and the money was surely going to run out at some point. We were back to square one – miles from the UK and with no escape route. To make matters worse, the handler didn't even seem to care. He'd got his money, so he was happy. When I looked over at him I realised he was fast asleep.

# CHAPTER 14

# Soran

We were all quiet on the van ride back to the camp. Missing out so narrowly felt so frustrating. The only person who seemed positive was Hussein, even though I knew he must be exhausted from all that walking.

We didn't get much sleep for the rest of the night, and it felt like hours before the sun finally came up. When I woke up properly, Mum was praying. I went to sit next to Dad to talk about last night. He said he wasn't sure trusting Ali Reza was the right thing after all.

We were all tired and grumpy that day. Hussein and I played around, distracting Hessam and keeping him busy. But all we wanted was to get to our safe haven. I just wished there was a way of helping Mum and Dad, a way of finally getting us out of here. Dad seemed stressed, and I knew he was desperately trying to think of a way we could try again. He didn't look like he could face another failure.

As soon as we were up Mum forced us to go and get some breakfast. It could be a long day, she said, and we needed to give Dad a break. Hussein and I followed Mum to the canteen, but Hessam wouldn't come and locked his arms around Dad's leg. Dad seemed a bit annoyed at this, but eventually agreed to take him off for a walk.

Returning from breakfast we found Dad and Hessam already back in our room. Dad's mood had changed from earlier that morning, and he seemed excited.

'What's happened?' asked Mum.

'We had a little meeting, didn't we, Hessam?' said Dad, ruffling Hessam's hair. He then went on to tell us how they had been walking through the market in the camp when they'd heard a voice calling out to them.

'I wasn't in the right mood for a chat,' said Dad, 'so I ignored it at first. But this guy wouldn't stop, so eventually I asked him what the hell he wanted. Well, he turned out to be the handler from last night.'

Mum's eyes widened. 'He's got a cheek,' she said.

'I know,' said Dad. 'But here's the thing. I was about to give him a piece of my mind when he said he was sorry.' When we all looked surprised Dad nodded. 'He apologised that it hadn't worked out and said he was really sorry we hadn't reached our destination.'

We were all amazed. That was the first time we'd ever heard of a handler actually caring about what happened to us. Normally they were ruthless. As long as they had their money they were happy.

'Turns out he is no ordinary handler,' Dad said. 'I asked him why he was apologising and he said that he'd still like to help us get across the border.'

'But we don't have any more money,' said Mum.

'I know. He said he'll do it for free. He said we'd already paid and the money we'd given him was for him to get us to our destination. So he's prepared to honour his agreement.'

Hussein and I looked at each other. We had thought that guy was a scumbag. 'Really? That has to be a joke, right?' Hussein said.

'He seemed pretty serious,' said Dad. 'He said that no matter what, promises are not meant to be broken. So he'd like to help us again.'

It seemed crazy – a human trafficker talking about not breaking promises and honouring his agreement? I couldn't believe it. After all we'd been through I'd doubted whether there were any good people at all, let alone handlers.

'It just goes to show,' said Mum. 'You can't judge a book by its cover.'

'What does that mean?' asked Hessam.

'It's a saying,' said Mum. 'It means that we often jump to conclusions and think people are one thing, when in reality they can be something totally different. Just because he's a handler doesn't mean he's a bad person.'

'So what do you think?' said Dad. 'Shall we trust him again?'

'What other choice is there?' said Mum.

Dad agreed, saying he'd repay his new-found faith in humanity by letting the handler honour his promise. I wasn't quite sure what he meant, but I thought it was that we'd be having another try.

We had a 'normal' day, whatever that was these days. We squabbled and played together, but always with the next step of our journey hanging over us. We tried not to think too much about what it would involve. What had happened in the field and with the dog had scared us all. Dad at least seemed less stressed. I think just having a plan helped. Whatever we had to do, we all knew that we were doing it for Hussein. If we didn't need to get medical help for him we could have settled in any one of the countries we'd been to so far. But it had to be the UK. Only there could we get the operation he needed. We had to keep going.

As morning became afternoon we started to think about what we might have to do. The story of the raft came into my head again but I tried not to think about it. I hoped there wouldn't be so much walking this time at least. Hessam said he didn't care as long as it wasn't so dark. Hussein didn't say much because he never complained as much as we did, but I knew he must be worried about all the walking too. I suddenly thought: what would we do if this attempt failed too? What if we ended up like Ali Reza, still here after fifteen failed attempts? I didn't think Hussein's heart would last that long.

As the afternoon wore on, Dad started to worry. He said he wondered whether he should have asked the handler some more questions, like what the attempt would involve. Mum said it couldn't be much worse than last night. And anyway, it was too late to get another handler. Dad said he needed to know. He was going to look for him in the camp – we needed to be prepared.

While Dad went off to find the handler we waited nervously for night time. Mum made us eat as much as we could so we'd be well prepared, and after that we just sat and waited. 'It might be a long night,' she said.

When Dad came back he was shaking his head in disbelief. Mum looked nervous.

'What's happened?' she said.

'I found out where the handler stays,' said Dad. 'You're not going to believe this, but I caught him packing away all his belongings!'

'He's doing a runner?' I asked.

Dad shook his head. 'No. That's the strange thing. He says he's sick of this life and wants to get away to the UK himself.'

We didn't understand. 'Why the change of heart?' said Mum. 'He must make good money doing this.'

'I think he does,' said Dad. 'But – you won't believe this – he says he wants to help us. I've no idea why, but he says he doesn't want people's money any more. He's tired of exploiting people. He just wants to help us to get to the UK.'

I wondered why anyone would want to exploit people anyway. But what Dad was saying seemed true: the handler wasn't such a bad guy after all. He wanted to help us because he liked us and felt sorry for Hussein, not because we'd paid him.

'So do we get our money back?' grinned Hussein.

Dad patted him on the head playfully. 'I doubt it! But he does promise he'll get us to the UK. This is his last trip, and he swears on his life it's going to work.'

'So what's the route?' asked Mum. Dad looked blank.

'I didn't ask!'

We all rolled our eyes at the thought of yet another night of unknown adventures. All we knew was that we were supposed to meet the handler later that night in the same place as last time. Dad told us we should get some rest first. This time, nothing was going to go wrong.

It was about midnight by the time we met the handler. Dad said he felt bad about leaving Ali Reza, but there was no way he was taking any risks this time, so it was just going to be us.

The handler said he had a 'different route', but he didn't tell us what it would be. He just took us out of the camp onto a different path, still as pitch black as the other one. I hoped it wasn't going to be a replay of last night. But this time he seemed to be on our side. Before we'd gone far he stopped and stooped down. 'Come on,' he said to Hussein. 'Get on.' Hussein couldn't believe it. A handler, offering him a piggyback? It seemed weird. 'We can't have you getting tired like last time,' he said.

After a bit of struggling and a lot of giggles as the handler tried to get Hussein up on his back, everyone felt warm and excited. Hussein wanted to thank him, and the handler said his name was Soran. It was definitely an improvement on the night before. Even though there was still a lot of walking, my legs didn't feel so heavy. I also didn't feel as scared as I had last night. I felt like we might even make it.

I didn't know whether I was imagining it, but as we walked along the path it seemed to be getting lighter. Then we went up and down a few slopes. The grass was much shorter than last night, which was a relief. Then the handler said we were getting closer and stopped to put Hussein down. 'Not far now,' he said.

We were getting tired and the last bit was uphill, but in the distance we could see a light – or maybe a set of lights – coming from the other side of the hill. As we got closer I realised the lights were coming from a road. They were streetlights, rows of them all along the side of a motorway. But there were no cars. Had Soran got us lost? Train tracks made sense, but an empty motorway didn't seem like it was going to get us out of here.

'What's next?' asked Dad as we got to the edge of the road.

'We need to cross over to the other side,' said Soran. As if it was simple.

'And then what? Thumb a ride?' I muttered. The place was deserted.

We followed Soran to a place where we could cross. Even though there were no cars in sight we still automatically looked both ways. It felt weird crossing what would normally be such a busy road. We walked halfway across to the middle section of the motorway. Here there were two big concrete blocks that separated the two sides. We waited again to make sure there weren't any invisible cars on the other side, then crossed the final few lanes.

When we got to the other side we didn't wait by the road like I thought we would but followed Soran away from it. Then I saw what he was heading for.

Ahead of us was a mass of huge metal boxes. Almost double my height, they were hard to miss, and I couldn't believe I hadn't seen them from the other side of the road.

'Let's go, it's almost time,' Soran said, and he led us into the maze of boxes. There were so many. We zigzagged between them as Soran stopped by each one as if to inspect it. I couldn't help but think it would be a fun place for hide-and-seek, if things were different.

As we went through more and more of the metal boxes, Soran was starting to look worried. Then he stopped still. Suddenly he smiled. What had he seen? He was putting his head against the closest rusty metal box now, just like the doctors used to when they listened to Hussein's heart. Then he waved his hand at us, which I think meant 'be quiet' and we all stood there, waiting.

Seemingly happy with his examination, Soran brought his ear away from the box. Then he did something weird. He knocked on the side of the box in a funny combination of short and long knocks, leaving a different length of pause between each one. What was this? Some sort of code?

We all waited. There was a pause and then Soran made a few more knocks. 'Step back,' he said. Suddenly there was a huge clunking noise from inside the rusty box, and the big metal locks started to move. It was like the box was unlocking all by itself. Before we knew it the doors had opened completely, and by the lights from the motorway behind us we could just see what was inside – and it looked like lots of pairs of eyes.

I guess we must have looked exactly like that when the French border guards found us hiding in the lorry. As I looked from person to person, each pair of eyes looked more terrified. There were so many of them – almost 50 – more than I would ever have guessed would fit into a box that size. They were crammed in the box like farm animals. Soran seemed to know some of them, and I wondered whether they were his trafficker friends, but they didn't seem to be expecting him. In fact, they all looked pretty surprised to see us.

Soran seemed keen to close the box again, so he started to push us towards it. Surely he didn't expect us to get in there too? It was full to the brim! There wasn't room for one more person, let alone six.

But that's what he told us to do. He said it was dangerous to be out in the open and we had to get out of sight. So one by one we squeezed into the box, finding room wherever we could. Soran pushed and arranged us so everyone could fit.

Once we were in, Soran made sure all our arms and legs were inside before he pulled the doors shut. To anyone on the outside, our box now looked exactly the same as all the others in the maze. It was like we'd disappeared.

As soon as we were locked in the box things started to get stressful. The other handlers in the box didn't seem too keen on our family being in there, and they were worried about having too many people to take care of. They had an angry argument with Soran, and I felt a bit sorry for him. We tried not to say anything.

I couldn't hear everything Soran was saying to them, but it sounded like he was promising he'd take responsibility for us. They were still cross, but it seemed to settle it.

While this was going on, I looked around me. The inside smelt of rust and iron, and all I could see in the dim light were the faces of people and families. I thought again how much they looked like us – scared but sort of hopeful at the same time. There were all ages, from babies to grandparents, and they looked like they came from all continents and religions. But inside that box we were all basically the same. We just wanted to get to our safe haven.

There was a lot of waiting inside the box. The good thing was that we didn't have to walk any more, but it was so cramped I felt like screaming. As time wore on the smell also worsened. After a while the other handlers started to choose people – every few minutes they'd point at a few people and open the box and take them out. I didn't know what happened to them after that.

Waiting to be chosen like this reminded me of the pit. But there we were out in the open and there were stars and bushes to go to the toilet in. Here, we were trapped inside a rusty box. I hoped this choosing game wouldn't be like last time. I hoped we wouldn't be the last to get picked.

'I beg you, don't leave us here,' Dad whispered to Soran.

'Don't worry,' he said, putting his hand on Dad's shoulder. 'I will be getting you and your family across this time.' He shook Dad's hand, as if that proved he was telling the truth. Dad shook his hand back and settled down next to us to wait.

The good thing about other families being taken out of the box was that it got emptier and emptier. We could finally stretch our legs around and breathe a bit more easily. Was it our turn soon? I worried that we'd be the last ones left.

Then: 'It's time,' said Soran suddenly. I wondered how he knew. But he spoke to one of the other handlers, checking some number with him, and then pushed us towards the rusty doors.

Hussein and I stood up. We were ready. We didn't know what for, but we were ready. As soon as the doors opened, Soran leapt out and we followed, the door clicking shut behind us. We were in the maze of other containers again, and Soran started sniffing around them like before.

He twisted and turned, stopping to check the numbers that were written on them. Why was he doing this? I didn't want to get out of one container and into another! Finally he seemed to find what he was looking for. He stopped at a particular container, but this time he didn't make funny knocks on it. He just fiddled with the locks, which made a quick snap, and then the doors to the container were open.

He and Dad pulled the rusty doors wide, and I peered anxiously inside. I hoped I wouldn't see more people. I really didn't want to be in someone's armpit again.

But there were no terrified eyes looking back at us. In fact, this container was full of what looked like cardboard boxes, piled high right up to the ceiling. There was just a little gap between the top of the boxes and the roof. Soran said that was where we were supposed to hide.

He didn't hang around. He got into the container, climbing through the cardboard boxes inside by hooking his hands into their handles. Then he dragged Dad up behind him, and once Dad was at the top he was able to help us and Mum to climb up too.

There was hardly any space. Soran told us to squeeze in between the top of the boxes and the ceiling, and we each found a place the best we could. 'Try and get comfortable,' Mum said, which I thought was a funny thing to say in the situation.

I then realised she meant that we might be in this con-tainer for a long time. It was a tiny space, and I really didn't want to be in here any longer than we had to be. I tried to 'get comfortable', but it was difficult as there wasn't even enough space between the boxes and the ceiling to sit. All we could do was lie down on top of the boxes, our faces flat up against the plastic lining of the ceiling.

'This is it,' said Soran, and I wondered what 'it' was. Were we going to be loaded onto a train? Or a boat? Whatever happened, I knew it could be a long time before we could get out, so I tried to get used to the situation. Mum, as usual, tried to keep us distracted. This time she started to talk about something she knew we all loved: food.

'What are we going to eat when we get there?' she asked us.

Without hesitating, I started to list all the meals I could think of. Hessam chose only puddings, and Hussein wanted burgers. He even mentioned pizza at one point.

Dad said he wanted traditional Afghan food, and even Soran joined in, although he said he didn't care what he ate, as long as it was something.

All this talk of food made me really hungry, and I won-dered when we would get any real food to eat. But at least it passed the time. Still, the night went on and on in the cold, rusty container, although I must have fallen asleep, because I don't remember very much after that.

The next thing I knew Mum was gently nudging me awake. As soon as I opened my eyes I started to ask her where we were, but she immediately shushed me. I listened. Outside the container I could hear the rumbling of heavy engines. It sounded like lorries.

They seemed to be driving around the maze of containers, loading them on for transportation. I could hear the huge clipping-in noise each time a box was loaded, and suddenly I was scared. Then there was the high-pitched noise of a lorry reversing, and Soran signalled to us not to make a noise.

A few more beeps and then we were jolted with a loud clang and a click. I'd seen these lorries before at the pit, and I thought this was when the lorry locked itself on to the container. Sure enough, suddenly our whole box rocked and shuddered. We were being loaded.

Did this mean we were on our way to our safe haven? It was exciting but terrifying at the same time. Would it be safe on the back of a lorry? What if we fell off? How long would it be before we could get out? Dad said he didn't know the answer to any of those questions. All we could do was hope everything would work out.

The shuddering stopped, and now we could just hear the rumble of the engine. Then we started to move. I was getting quite good at guessing what was happening in moving vehicles by now, and I worked out that we'd driven out of the maze of boxes and onto some tarmac. Everything felt smoother and we were picking up speed.

Dad suddenly seemed to realise something. He looked at Soran. 'How do you know where this lorry is going?' he said quickly.

Soran looked a bit guilty. 'I don't exactly … I have intel that says it's heading to the port, but …'

'What?' said Dad, suddenly furious. 'So we could be going in the wrong direction?' After all that we could be heading back into Europe, or towards the Middle East.

'It will be fine,' said Soran, but I could tell by his face that he wasn't so sure.

Mum tried to calm Dad, saying that we couldn't do much about it now anyway. We just had to trust and pray that we were heading for the port and across to the UK.

I felt the lorry picking up more speed, and I wondered if that was a bad sign. Surely the port wouldn't be far from here? But after a while it started to slow down again, and I felt that we might be about to stop. Soran looked relieved too.

I was right. After a few minutes the lorry came to a complete stop, then it juddered forward slowly and we started to hear voices. 'This must be the port!' said Hussein.

Mum and Dad looked worried. I knew why. It wasn't as simple as just sailing right across to the UK from here. If we were at the port then that meant a security checkpoint, and that meant that anyone could open up the container and check what was inside. Here was where it could all go wrong.

At this point Soran wriggled over to Mum and Dad to give them a lot of instructions. They didn't make a lot of sense to me, but I hoped Mum and Dad got what he meant.

The lorry kept on creeping forward. Then it stopped again, and we could hear the driver talking to someone. We must be at the checkpoint. He was answering questions, and I knew that if they were going to open up the container, now would be the time.

Then Dad told us to do something strange. 'You're going to have to hold your breath for a bit,' he said.

'What? Why?' Hussein asked. Having to hold his breath always sent him into a panic.

'It's okay,' said Dad. 'Soran says the security guards have machines, that's all. They can measure the amount of carbon dioxide in the container – that's the gas we make when we breathe out. If there's lots of carbon dioxide then it shows that there might be stowaways.'

I took a big gulp of air. I held it for as long as I could, my cheeks puffed out like balloons, but I really wanted to let it out and take another breath. I could hear a few more checks going on, some beeps, and then Dad signalled to us that we could breathe again.

The lorry started to move, slowly, and Soran looked relieved. I looked over at Hussein to check he was okay, but he looked pink enough and I couldn't hear him rasping. So far so good.

We felt some more rumbling and going over what felt like ramps and then we were heading up a slope. After that the engine went off and the lorry driver stopped and turned off the engine. We must be on the ferry.

I'd looked at enough maps to know that there was now just a little bit of sea between us and our safe haven. Probably only a few hours to get across. I wondered what the UK was actually like. And if we'd even get there. And whether that would mean Hussein could get better.

# CHAPTER 15

# Inside the container

Once we were on the ferry things started to get worse inside the container. We knew we still had a long way to go before we would get fresh air, and it was becoming really stuffy. Hussein didn't complain, but I knew he must be struggling as the air felt really thin. It was smelly too, and Hessam started to whinge, saying that he couldn't breathe and that he was hungry. We were all hungry. It was so many hours since we'd had a meal, and it was hard to tell how long we'd been in the container. I started to feel panicky.

Dad wriggled over to Soran again and asked him how much longer he thought it would be. 'The kids are suffering,' he said. Then Hessam started to cry. I just wished we could feel the rumble of engines again. That would mean we were on our way.

Suddenly Hessam made a funny noise, and Dad wriggled over to him. But it was too late. I heard him retch, then retch again, and then he threw up all over the boxes we were lying on. The smell was disgusting, and for a minute I thought I was going to throw up as well. My stomach felt so empty.

Mum was trying to get across to Hessam now, but because we were in such a small space she couldn't reach him. Dad had managed to crawl over to him and comfort him, but he kept on crying.

'There's got to be a way to get some more air into this place,' said Mum, desperately. We all looked around. I just wanted to get away from that smell. I looked at the door of the container. That wouldn't work. It was too heavy, and if anyone saw it open we'd be found out.

Then Dad said he had an idea. He pointed at the roof of the container. It wasn't metal, like the sides, but a sort of plastic sheeting, a bit like the roof of the lorry back in the Netherlands. I remembered Dad slashing it with the knife so we could get in. 'Find something sharp,' he said.

We looked around, but we didn't have anything with us that would work. Soran even tried to open some of the huge boxes we were lying on to see if he could find something sharp enough to cut through the plastic. Hessam was gasping for air now – I think being sick had made him panic. Mum looked worried. 'Hurry,' she said. 'He can't breathe.'

We were all panicking now. I knew people died in these containers, especially little kids. We searched around frantically on top of the boxes. Then suddenly Dad said, 'Got something!' He'd made his way over to the corner of the container, and he started to crawl back as quickly as he could. He'd found a long nail, probably from where the plastic was nailed down to the sides. It looked pretty sharp.

Before I knew it he'd started attacking the lining on top of the container above Hessam, pushing the sharp tip of the nail through the thick material until suddenly we could see daylight. A tiny bit of cool breeze came in, then more as he made the hole bigger. As Hessam breathed the oxygen flooding into the container the colour started to come back into his face. I felt better too.

Dad made a few more holes to let as much air into the container as he could without someone noticing it. I breathed in deeply. Not long after we heard the rumble of the engine that we had been waiting for. We were moving.

Now the only problem we had was hunger. There was no way Dad was going to be able to solve that, unless we happened to be lying on boxes of takeaway, so we just had to try to ignore our rumbling tummies. We lay there, waiting for some sound that would show us we were reaching the other side.

After what felt like hours we started to feel the ferry slow down and the louder propellers working. Then we could hear people talking and getting to their cars, and not long after that I could hear the lorry drivers talking on their phones and turning on their radios. We're here, I thought.

I had a tingling feeling in my tummy, like nerves. Was this it? Finally, were we in the UK? I knew that we just had to get on to British soil and we'd be okay, but I couldn't help worrying that something else was going to go wrong in the meantime.

Suddenly we heard a louder noise, like grinding metal, and Mum said it was the mechanical gates opening. That meant we'd docked. I heard the lorry driver put the lorry into gear, and before long we were moving off slowly, with a radio blaring. We were definitely somewhere, but were we in the right country? Soran said we had to be patient and wait a bit longer so we were clear of the authorities. But we didn't feel patient. I needed the toilet so badly, and we were all weak from hunger. It felt like we'd been in that container for days.

Hussein and I kept looking over at Soran for any sign that it was okay to move, but still he shook his head. We can't get it wrong now, he told us.

Finally, the lorry seemed to be picking up speed, and I knew we must be on a motorway. I asked Soran if we were far enough away from the port by now. He said maybe. Dad said it was time to get out of here. I couldn't have agreed more.

It turned out that getting out of the container was easier said than done. Somehow, after spending hours staying as quiet as we could, now we had to get the attention of the driver. But we were on a motorway and he was playing loud music, so we were going to have to make a lot of noise to be heard above the racket. Soran was the closest to the driver's cab, so he started to kick the metal box with his heels. We joined in and started screaming and shouting to make as much noise as we could.

We went on screaming and kicking like this for a while, and it took a lot of our energy. That we'd had no food or water since our last meal in the camp wasn't helping. After a while Mum said she didn't think it was any good – the lorry driver still couldn't hear us.

I wondered what else we could do, and thought back to *Knight Rider*. What would he have done? Dad had a white handkerchief, and, remembering something else I'd seen on

TV in Moscow, I pushed it out of one of the holes in the top of the container, a sign of peace. It didn't work.

We were all getting tired now, and I didn't think I could kick and scream for much longer. But what else could we do?

Then Dad remembered the nail he'd used earlier to puncture the hole in the plastic. He shouted to Soran, who was taking a break from his own kicking. Passing the nail to him, Dad made a sign to tell Soran to scrape it on the metal. Soran did it, and the nail started making a high-pitched noise on the side of the container. It was quite loud. Perhaps that would work? All we needed was for the driver to think there was something wrong with the lorry and stop to check it out.

Suddenly something changed. 'Shhh,' said Soran. We listened. The music had got quieter. The lorry driver must have turned it down. Now was our chance. We all started screaming and kicking as loudly as we could, banging and banging on the side of the container. He must have heard us this time, because straight away we felt the lorry brake sharply. Then we felt it swing off the motorway and come to a stop. Was this it? The end of being on the run?

Just as this happened, Hussein suddenly started gasping for breath. It must have been all the kicking and shouting, as well as the lack of oxygen in the container. His heart was having to work harder than ever. Mum took hold of him to try to calm him down. She started praying quietly and telling Hussein to take long, slow breaths. Eventually his breathing started to regulate.

Dad told us to stay quiet now and we listened. We heard the driver's door slam shut and could hear his heavy footsteps towards the back of the lorry. My tummy fluttered. Then there was the clunk of the heavy metal doors, and we all held our breath as we waited for them to open. We'd been in that box of death for over 24 hours and I couldn't wait to get out, but part of me was terrified of what we'd find on the other side of the door. What if we were in the wrong country? What if they sent us straight back to Calais? It couldn't go wrong now, it just couldn't.

As the door creaked open daylight started to come through the gap. We all blinked. We'd been in darkness for so long that it felt like being blinded. Then I could see the driver's face as he peered in among the boxes. It was a familiar sight, not because I knew him, but because I'd seen those facial expressions before. At first he looked confused, because he'd heard a noise but all he could see in the lorry were the long cardboard boxes he was transporting. Then I sat up. As he locked eyes on me his expression turned from confusion to surprise. There was something else on board.

I couldn't climb down from where I was, and I was too scared to anyway, so I waited for the driver to spot Dad and Soran before I did anything else. As the lorry driver saw that there were more of us his expression changed again, this time back to confusion. Just like the lorry driver in France, he couldn't work out how so many people had sneaked onto his lorry without him noticing.

The adults started to make their way towards the door then, but as they did the driver started to get angry. He started shouting at us in a language I didn't know, and I guessed it must be pretty annoying to think you're delivering boxes when actually you're doing something illegal. Plus, it stank of sick in there.

Hussein, Hessam and I quickly followed Dad down the cardboard boxes and jumped into his arms. The driver kept shouting at us, and Dad made us all hurry to the side of the motorway. Once we were out, for a minute the driver didn't seem to know what to do. Then he said something under his breath that was probably a swear word before taking one last check inside the container. Happy that there were no more stowaways, he hurried back to his cab and got in. He didn't waste any time driving away, and I thought he was a bit of a coward. Why wouldn't he help us? Mum said he had no choice – if he called the police he'd be arrested.

So that was it. Once again we were stranded at the side of the motorway in a foreign country. We didn't even know if we were in the UK. How could we find out? We could hardly stop the cars and ask them where we were. We didn't even speak English. One of the only words we knew was 'refugees', along with 'hello' and 'thank you'.

But it was good to be out of that container. I felt my lungs quickly filling with air, and although I was still starving hungry, I felt better straight away. But the fresh air had another effect. Suddenly I remembered how desperately I needed to pee. We hadn't been to the toilet since being in the container, and getting out into the fresh air made me need it more than ever.

I ran over to Dad, and it turned out he and the others had just had the same feeling. With no toilets and not even any bushes to hide in, we had no choice. Soran told us to make a big circle and stand with our backs to each other. Mum said he looked like he'd done that before. She walked off, saying she didn't want anything to do with it. But Hussein and

Hessam and I found it hilarious, and we started giggling uncontrollably. That made us need to pee even more, and we made a big circle just like Soran had said. As I emptied my bladder the relief was amazing.

Then some of the cars started to beep their horns. 'I think we must be in the UK, Dad,' I said. 'Look how friendly they are.'

Dad winced. But then he seemed to realise something. 'Look at the cars,' he said, pointing at the traffic whizzing past. 'Look where the drivers are sitting.'

At first I didn't know what he meant, but then I realised that the drivers were all on the wrong side of the car. Isn't that the thing about the UK? They drive on the other side? Mum came back and put her hands over her mouth. Then she made a funny noise. Dad grabbed her and they stood there, crying.

Then Dad turned to us. All these months, all the drama and all the travelling, he said, had finally been worth it. We were here. Our safe haven. 'This is it boys,' he added, smiling. 'No more running away.'

I couldn't believe it. After all the adventures, here we were. It was amazing, but hard to get used to. Did that mean things were going to be okay now? Here, at the side of a motorway with cars whizzing past us? Here, where we'd just peed on the road? I guessed it didn't matter. The main thing was to get to the UK. The fact that we were starving hungry and had no idea when we were going to get some food didn't matter. It felt good to be here.

Then Soran said what we were all thinking: we needed to find a way off this road. We started to walk along the empty lane at the side of the motorway, and eventually we came to a service station. In the distance I could see what I knew were signs for fast food shops, and my tummy began rumbling harder than ever. But Dad looked worried, and I suddenly realised we had no money.

Then Soran did something really kind. He pulled Dad to one side and showed him some notes in his pocket. He had money! I remembered all those times I'd hated him at the beginning and felt embarrassed. He might be a handler but he was definitely a good guy.

Eating hot food after so long with no food at all was the best feeling ever. Smothering everything with the little sachets of ketchup, we ate anything we could get our hands on. Straight away we started to feel better. The last time I'd felt this happy was at the camp with the football field, and I looked around at Mum with pride. She read my mind. 'We've been through a lot to get here,' she said. I nodded, food still in my mouth. 'It just goes to show, Hamed, what happens when we don't give up.'

After we'd eaten it was time to work out what to do. We didn't know where we were, and even if we had it wouldn't have meant much to us. How were we supposed to get to the authorities? We could hardly walk up to the service station staff and say 'refugees'.

Dad asked Soran what we should do. But he shook his head. 'I'm sorry,' he said, 'but here is where we have to say goodbye.' We all looked at him. Goodbye? Why did he have to go? We'd got so used to his help that I'd almost forgotten he wasn't a part of our family. But his mind was made up – he needed to make his own way now.

I looked at Hussein. He and Soran had become quite close over the last few days. He looked sad. 'It's okay, bro,' said Soran, borrowing my nickname for Hussein. 'You've got some work to do to get better now.' He put his hand on Hussein's heart and winked. Then he turned to Dad. 'I hope he gets a doctor soon,' he whispered.

It wasn't just weird saying goodbye to Soran, it was worrying. We'd relied on him for so much on this trip that it didn't feel good to be on our own. As he walked off out of the service station I wondered where he would go and what would happen to him. 'He'll be fine,' said Mum.

Dad got back to business. 'We need to find the local police,' he said. He told us we needed to look out for anything that looked official, like a police car or uniform, and with our tummies finally full this felt like an adventure. We went out onto the tarmac and looked around. But none of the cars there looked like police cars, just people going on holiday. So Dad said we would just have to walk until we found someone.

As plans went it wasn't very good. We'd set off down the motorway and try to get off it and into a town. There we might be able to find a police station. After walking along the empty lane for a bit we found an exit and eventually it became a smaller road. Then we were on regular streets and there started to be shops and houses. But we were exhausted. I couldn't remember the last time I'd slept and the full tummy was starting to wear off. No one talked much.

Not knowing where we were going or who we could turn to, we just kept on walking for miles in the hope that Dad's plan would fall into place. The joy of finding our safe haven started to become a distant memory as us boys bickered and jostled with each other. I got sick of looking at Hessam's whingeing face and got more and more angry each time he tripped me up.

As day started to turn into evening, we were all really hungry. There really was no money this time, as Soran didn't have enough to leave us any before he went. We kept passing shops that looked like they sold food, but how could we go in and ask for it if we had no way of paying?

Dad said we had no choice, and that he had heard a lady on TV called Oprah say 'You get in life what you have the courage to ask for'. So, trying to be brave, we went into each of the shops and asked at the counter if they could spare anything as we didn't have any money. At first I found this embarrassing, but Mum said everyone had a bad day now and then, and it was always okay to ask for help.

Shop after shop politely told us no, they couldn't give us something for nothing. But then something happened that changed everything. Just as we came out of the third shop, Dad felt a tap on the shoulder. He turned around, and was greeted by a big, kind smile. It was a man in uniform. Police!

Crying with joy, Dad took hold of his shoulders. 'Refugees,' he said, pointing at us. 'Refugees.'

# CHAPTER 16

# Safe

The kind policeman got us some food. Then he arranged for a van to come and get us, and as we waited Dad kept saying that he knew it would be like this eventually. This was why we called it a safe haven. He seemed pleased that all our hard work had paid off.

Our tummies full again, we got into the van and watched colourful shops pass the window while we were taken to the refugee processing centre. On the way, Dad and Mum talked about how they should tell the police about Hussein's illness. Neither of them could speak English, and it was a complicated thing to describe. But he was looking weaker than ever after the journey in the container, and I couldn't believe how pale he was. They needed to say something now.

Sitting in the front seat, Dad kept turning to the policeman, and I could tell that he was trying to think of how to explain Hussein's situation. But when the policeman saw him looking and asked him something in English, all Dad could manage to say was 'thank you'. The driver smiled and put his hand on Dad's shoulder.

Eventually the van came to a huge building with white walls and a big metal gate. We stopped at the gate and the policeman had to wait to be buzzed in. Inside it was like a compound, and the van stopped. The policeman helped us out and made sure we were okay. Then he took us to a waiting room, where he shook hands with Dad before going back to duty. Suddenly we didn't feel so safe. The other policemen and women didn't seem so friendly, and I wished the first guy would come back.

Then a new policeman came over and said something in English. He kept asking Dad questions, but they didn't seem to realise we couldn't understand. All Dad could do was keep saying 'refugee', but the policeman asking the questions was just getting annoyed. Eventually another policeman started saying names, and after a while we realised he was listing countries. 'They're asking where we're from,' said Mum.

'Ah,' said Dad. 'Afghan, Afghanistan – Afghani.' The policeman seemed relieved. He said something to the other policemen and I heard the word again: 'Afghanistan'. They looked back at Dad and he nodded to confirm. The policeman said something else, but it all sounded like an alien language.

Then one of them came back to us and said slowly, 'Farsi or Pashto?' and Dad nodded quickly. 'Farsi,' he said. He turned to us and put his thumbs up. Success!

But then things started to feel less positive. One of the policemen came back over and asked Dad to stand in front of him. He looked cross. Then he started patting Dad with both hands down the sides of his body, just like I'd seen police do to criminals on the TV. But Dad wasn't a criminal! What did they think we had? A gun? Next it was Mum's turn, and then they even searched each of us, as if Hessam was going to have a hidden revolver down in his trousers. It felt horrible.

Eventually the police seemed happy that we weren't carrying any weapons, so one of them took us down a bright corridor with white, shiny walls. The floor squeaked as we walked on it. At the end of the corridor was a set of blue metal doors with big handles. I wondered if this was what prison was like.

We stopped by the doors and the policeman unlocked them and pointed inside. Hessam looked scared. 'Dad,' he whimpered, but I held on to him so he'd be quiet.

'It's okay,' said Dad and nodded and smiled. He told us to go into the room, so we all trooped in. It really was like a prison. The room was bright white just like the corridor and there was no window. In the corner was a metal container which, when I looked closer, turned out to be a toilet. A toilet in a box! We've been arrested, I thought.

The policeman told us boys to sit down and he pointed to a solid shelf with a thin blue layer of material on top of it. Hessam asked if it was a bed and I giggled – until I realised that it was.

Then the policeman said something else to Dad in English and went out of the room, shutting and locking the metal doors behind us.

'Why do I feel like we're in prison?' said Hussein as soon as he'd gone.

'Because we are,' I said.

Hessam panicked then and asked if we were baddies. Mum shushed him and said no, it was probably just to give us somewhere to go.

We sat on the hard bed while Mum and Dad paced round the room. I started to joke about the toilet in a box to Hussein, wanting to lighten the mood and stop everyone from looking so serious. But we all still felt worried. Thankfully we were also really tired, so it didn't take much for us to fall asleep.

The next thing I knew was the clunking of the metal lock again. Mum went to the door and a different police-man handed her some plastic trays. Mum said thank you and brought the trays into the room. As soon as I saw the food I realised how hungry I was, and we ate what was on them quickly. As the policeman left I noticed that he didn't lock the door this time. Mum noticed too. 'So we're not criminals after all,' she said to Dad. She was stressed, and I knew it was just because she was worried about what was coming next, especially for Hussein.

We had to stay in the cell for another few hours, and then suddenly we heard the door creak open again. It was the same policeman who'd brought the food. He said something short to Dad in English, but none of us understood, and it looked like he wanted us to follow him. We felt cautious, but we got up and followed him out of the room. Mum kept us very close to her as we walked down the bright white corridors again.

We passed more blue metal doors, and I wondered whether there were real criminals behind them. It didn't look much like the prisons I'd seen on TV. It made me feel nervous though. When we got to a set of big doors the policeman swiped a card and it beeped, then he pushed them and we went through. On the other side there were a few more policemen, and they looked like they were waiting for us. I noticed there was someone else there as well, and he wasn't in uniform. He was smiling and looked a bit friendlier than the others.

After all our travels in the boots of cars, lorries and metal containers, a friendly, smiling face was an amazing thing to see. We all smiled back. When we got to the group the man said, '*Salam,* brother, *hale shoma khobeh?*' and I suddenly realised I could understand what he was saying! He was a translator, he spoke Farsi and he was asking how we were.

We couldn't believe it. Dad told him we were all ok, but we'd been put in a cell and had no idea what was going to happen to us. The man said he was sorry about that – they'd called him as soon as they'd worked out where we were from and he'd come as soon as he could. Dad seemed a bit speech-less with emotion then – maybe at hearing his own language spoken by an official for the first time in months – so Mum thanked the man for coming and said we were grateful.

Then we were taken by the translator to a different room, this time a much more colourful one with toys and proper seats. They brought us another tray with some water and sandwiches on it, so we ate as much as we needed. Then the translator took Dad into a separate room to talk to him. Before he did he asked Mum and Dad if they would like a tea or coffee. Dad told him we hadn't any money left at all. The translator smiled and said not to worry, it was all free. So they brought Mum some tea and Dad took his into the other room with the translator, whose name was Ali.

There was a big glass window between the two rooms, so we could see Dad through there with Ali while we played with the things in the first room. Every now and then I looked through. Dad seemed to be talking a lot, while Ali didn't say so much but made notes on a piece of paper. I hoped Dad was finally telling him about Hussein.

Dad was with Ali for ages, and a policewoman brought them several more cups of tea before they were finished. We were getting bored, so we were glad when Dad finally came back through. Mum looked at him expectantly.

'We've gone through everything,' he sighed. 'Why we had to leave, the details of the journey, all about Hussein,' said Dad. 'They understand that we need to see a doctor – or most likely a specialist – and fairly quickly. They're going to find us somewhere to spend the night now.'

I was relieved we weren't going to have to sleep in the prison cell with the toilet in a box. We got ready to go and Dad shook hands with Ali and even gave him a hug. He looked like he was going to cry again, and Hussein and I looked the other way as it was a bit embarrassing. Hessam asked Dad if he was okay, and Dad said yes, of course he was – he was just so grateful that we'd finally got here. I guessed it had been even more stressful for Dad than it had been for us. He was the one who always had to come up with a plan and make decisions. We just did what we were told. There must have been moments when he thought we wouldn't make it here. I suddenly realised how much responsibility you had to take when you were a dad.

Ali told us there was a van waiting, but before we left Dad asked him to thank the policeman who found us. 'He was very kind,' Dad said. Ali said he would, and we all went outside to find the van.

In the van Mum and Dad talked about Hussein some more and Dad told Mum what he had said to Ali. They seemed obsessed with finding Hussein a specialist now. I looked out of the windows at the people on the streets as we drove past them. Hussein was quiet.

'What's up, bro?' I asked.

'Just thinking,' he said.

'About what?'

'About how they're going to make me better,' he said. 'I don't want things to get bad. I always want it to be like this.'

'What, like *this*?' I giggled, pointing at the van. But Hussein was being serious.

'No, just … I don't know. All of us together. The circle. Happy.'

'It will, bro,' I said.

'Yeah, I'll make sure it will,' he said, 'I'm going to get better you know.' He pulled a funny face. Then he changed the subject, and we started to talk about what our new 'home' would look like. Hessam said he hoped the toilet wouldn't be in a box.

Before we knew it the van started to slow down and we seemed to be arriving. Wherever we were, I wondered how we'd talk to people, as Ali had gone and we didn't have a translator. It felt lonely, not understanding the people around us.

We pulled up to some metal gates, and through them I could see a huge building with tall glass windows. There was a sort of living room inside, and we could see the lights on. It looked warm and cosy compared to the grey skies outside.

Mum said it wasn't a living room – it was called a lobby. We got out of the van and a friendly-looking man met us with a smile. He showed us into the building and we realised that there were lots of other families there too. It was a sort of compound, and it felt friendly and lively. There were lots of other kids, and I wondered what their story was and how they'd got here. Mum and Dad had to fill in some paperwork then, and we waited to be shown to our accommodation. The staff were volunteers, Dad said, and some of them even spoke Farsi.

When all the forms were filled in they gave Dad a key, and he waved it in front of us. The key to our room! Mum laughed like she couldn't believe it. I couldn't either, and Hussein and Hessam and I danced round in excitement. We had to find the room, which had a number like in a hotel, and we went up the stairs and through corridors until we found some big oak doors with a golden door handle. As Dad opened the door the first thing I noticed was the smell of clean carpets and pillows. The sun had come out now and was coming in through the cream-coloured curtains. There were two double beds and some bunk beds, and we raced to them and squabbled over who got the top.

Mum found a kettle and some different teas. 'I can't remember the last time I made tea for my family,' she laughed.

Dad grinned. 'Go ahead then, I'd love one.' Mum rolled her eyes. Dad said he was only joking and told her to go and sit down while he made *her* tea. She didn't have to be asked twice, and went and sat down with us while Dad filled the kettle.

We'd found a little TV and were playing around with it, trying to get a channel. Outside the window we could see the sea, stretching out back towards France. Mum said she couldn't believe we'd come all that way in a metal container.

We spent the rest of the afternoon in the room and eventually fell asleep in the comfy beds to the sound of Mum and Dad murmuring and the TV on quietly in the background. It felt like home.

The next day we woke to the sun again. It was hard to get up as I was still so tired from the journey, but Mum promised there would be breakfast, so we soon got dressed. Downstairs it was just like a hotel in one of the movies we'd seen in Moscow – you had to get a tray and then you could help yourself to anything you wanted. Then you had to sit down at one of the hundreds of chairs and tables in the huge hall. It was the first hot breakfast I'd had in ages.

You had to do the same for lunch, and after this the staff told us we could go outside if we wanted. But we preferred to stay in our room where it was safe. We didn't know anything about England and I think we were all a bit scared of not knowing the language or culture. We'd only ever lived under the Taliban or been on the run, and I couldn't imagine what it would be like to live somewhere free. We also didn't know whether people would accept us. We were 'refugees' after all. Inside the compound felt safer.

What we didn't know was that, while we were hiding out in the compound by the sea, the British government was making decisions for us – about where we'd go, what we'd do, and what would happen to Hussein. Soon we'd find out what our future would be.

# CHAPTER 17

# Home

When I asked Dad how they decided where everyone would end up, he said that it depended on your preferred location, whether you were a family or single person and how much 'capacity' there was. I didn't understand what the last thing was, and I wondered how we were supposed to have a preferred location when we'd only just got here? He didn't mention hospitals either, but obviously they were going to send us somewhere with good doctors. Obviously.

After a few days Mum and Dad were called into a room with someone from the government and a translator from the compound. Was this it? Were we finally going to find out where our new home was? They were in there for ages, and at first I was worried that there'd been a mistake and they were sending us back to Afghanistan, but then Mum and Dad came out of the room and called us over.

'We're going to a city called Cardiff,' said Mum excitedly. 'We're going to be leaving soon.'

It didn't mean much to us. We'd no idea where Cardiff was or what it was like. But for Hussein, only one thing mattered. 'Are there good doctors there?' he asked.

Mum looked at Dad. He didn't seem to want to look her in the eye. She turned back to Hussein. 'Yes,' she said quickly. 'The doctors will be waiting for you there.'

I wasn't sure I believed her. Why did she look at Dad like that? And why were they in that room for so long? I hated not being told information. Had the government people really said the doctors were waiting for us, or did Mum just say that so Hussein wouldn't worry?

I decided to lighten the mood. 'We'll pack our things!' I said. This had become our family joke – we hadn't had any things to pack for months. Everyone laughed, and I saw Mum looking at Hussein. He did seem relieved. For the first time in my life I thought that telling lies might not always be bad.

The morning flew by and we ate our final lunch in the canteen. Excited about going to Cardiff, we kept asking the volunteers what they knew about it. What was there? What did it look like? After a while Mum told us to be quiet as there were other people in this compound – people who'd been here for longer than us – who still hadn't been told they had a new home. We were the lucky ones. I hadn't thought of it like that.

Eventually it was time to leave, and a volunteer came to get us to tell us that the minibus was waiting outside. I started to feel anxious as well as excited. What would it be like? Would there really be help for Hussein? I couldn't bear the thought of his disappointed face if there wasn't.

Before we left we looked around the compound at the people left behind. All those strangers, Mum said to us, even though they're from different countries and different beliefs, all have something in common with us. Hessam asked what it was and she said, 'Feelings. They all feel exactly the same as we do: scared, lonely and anxious about the future. No matter how far they've come or what they've been through, they all want the same things as us. They just want to belong.'

Then Dad said we had to go, so we said goodbye to the volunteers and walked out of the compound, leaving all those other people behind us. I guessed we really were the lucky ones.

Although we were setting off on another journey, this time it was different. Hopefully this was the last trip we'd make for a while, and hopefully Cardiff was the safe haven we'd been waiting for. We were all quiet as we sat in the van, thinking about how we'd fit in. I wondered how I'd ever learn the language or get used to the weather. It seemed to change every five minutes.

Hussein said he hoped there was somewhere to play football. He grinned at me, but I suddenly realised that I couldn't imagine him being able to play football any more. The dusty alleyway in Herat felt a million years ago, and Hussein was so much weaker now. *What's happened to my brother?* I wondered. I didn't know whether Hussein really did think he'd be able to play football or whether he was just saying this to be strong.

He must have known how ill he was. I promised myself that, somehow, I'd get him playing football again.

It was a long journey, and I think I fell asleep, as the next thing I knew was Dad's voice saying, 'Wakey wakey, sleepy heads.' I was annoyed to be woken up, but Dad said we were nearly there and when I looked out of the window, yawning and with bleary eyes, I saw trees and fields. I hadn't seen trees like that since the jungle in Ukraine. It was so green!

Soon we came off the motorway and into what looked like a big city. The buildings were very colourful and we started to approach what looked like a huge castle. Hessam asked if that was our new home, and we all laughed. But as we pulled up I could see more greenery and a play area, and I started to wonder whether we really had been made into kings and queens. Mum said she couldn't believe we were going to be able to just wander around without fear of the Taliban. 'No curfew either,' she said.

As we got out of the van there were more volunteers, and they all seemed friendly and nice. Although we'd talked about a 'safe haven' so much on the trip, I'd never really been able to imagine what it would be like. Now I realised this was it.

The volunteers told us to go towards the main entrance, and there we entered a main hall where there were other families and translators speaking different languages. We were such a mix of people – mostly mums, dads and children – but we had all made the journey here from different places.

Someone called our surname and Mum and Dad looked over. A kind-looking old man waved to us and shook Dad's hand. Then he tapped Hussein on the head and said, 'We've been waiting for you.' I wondered if he was the doctor.

He couldn't have been, because then he took us up some stairs and showed us a locked door. He had a big bunch of shiny keys and he stopped and gave a set to Mum and Dad. 'These are your keys,' he said, and nodded towards the door. Taking them, Dad turned the right one in the lock, our lock.

Behind the door wasn't just a room. There was an apartment, with different rooms, all for us. Unlike in the compound, we didn't race inside, ready to jump on our beds. We just stood in the doorway and looked in. We'd been trying to get here for so long it suddenly felt a bit weird. It had been so long since we had separate rooms, all to ourselves. This was our new place. Not for a day or a week, or a few months, but for as long as we wanted. This was where we were going to go to school and play and grow up. It was where Hussein was going to get better. This was home.

# CHAPTER 18

# The Three Musketeers

Those first few days were a blur. We just had to concentrate on getting used to our new home, the people in the neighbourhood and the city around us. The fact that this place was permanent meant that we felt more like exploring than we had at the compound, but we were still cautious. Everything that had happened on the journey here – from being robbed that first time in the market to being held at gunpoint on the motorway – had made us nervous of people we didn't know. I'd learnt not to trust anyone. If anyone was kind to us, I automatically wondered what they wanted in return.

The one thing we hadn't thought about was our education. We'd been on the road for so long and missed so much that I'd forgotten what school was even like. Hessam had barely been to any lessons at all before we left Afghanistan. So we were surprised when, after a few days in our new flat,

Mum and Dad called us in to the sitting room to 'talk about school'. I thought they'd just tell us that we'd need to start thinking about it. But Mum had it all already arranged. She said we'd been accepted into a local school and would be starting the following week.

My first thought was fear – which meant 'run'. How would we speak the language? What if everyone made fun of us? Would we be able to do the work? There were so many terrifying things I didn't know the answer to. Mum and Dad said they couldn't answer those questions. So I tried another one. 'Would Hussein and I be in the same class?' Dad said he'd see what he could do.

Before we could start, Mum and Dad had to do a lot of paperwork. There were two schools to sort out, as Hessam would be going to the local primary school while Hussein and I would go to the secondary comprehensive. Dad would sit at the dining table in the flat, papers everywhere, and I could tell by his body language that he was getting overwhelmed. I realised that we'd all been so focused on getting to the safe haven that none of us had thought about how we'd manage when we were here. Getting to the UK had been hard enough; living here at times seemed impossible.

Luckily, Mum and Dad had help. Volunteers and people who visited from the government department helped us with everything from filling in forms to finding a supermarket. I couldn't believe so many people wanted to help us for free. My memories of Afghanistan were only of the Taliban, who didn't help anyone. All they were interested in was making rules and punishing the people who didn't keep them. I thought that living in the UK must have been a relief for

Mum, as she no longer had to have a chaperone and stay in after dark, but Mum said she just worried about all the women left behind.

Every time someone from the government department came to help us Dad would say, 'And that's why we always called it a safe haven.' It got a bit annoying, as if he had to prove he was right all along! But we'd never stopped trusting him. One day, one of the volunteers gave Dad an envelope with green pieces of paper inside. Dad was confused. It wasn't money, but it looked a bit like it. The lady said they were vouchers. They were to spend on food and clothes from certain shops. We couldn't believe it. No one outside our family had ever given us money before. Except Soran.

I remembered the day, over a year ago, when we'd held the bazaar at our house, and people from our neighbourhood had come to buy all our belongings. We hadn't had anything of our own since then. Even the things we took with us had got lost, stolen or left along the way. Mum said the vouchers meant we'd be able to buy our own things. We'd be able to choose what food we ate, not just have to put up with whatever we were given. I hoped that might mean no more sandwiches. We'd had a lot of those.

The more I learnt about the UK government the more I realised how different it was to the Taliban. Obviously, I knew it was different – there were no executions for a start. But it still felt odd that a country would give its money to people who'd travelled from thousands of miles away – people who weren't even from the UK and had nothing to give in return. Mum said what goes around comes around, and we never knew when we might be able to repay the debt.

Dad slept better the day we got the vouchers. He seemed more relaxed, funnier, more like he used to be. The next morning he said, 'Who wants to go shopping? You'll need some uniform for your new schools.'

Mum was more excited than us. She loved education. She said that school was the best thing for children, and that we'd finally have some routine. We'd finally be normal kids. Back home so many people didn't get this opportunity, so it was important that we made the most of it.

We went to the shops with a few other families whose kids were also starting school. We giggled a lot as we tried on trousers and shirts, jumpers and ties. They weren't like anything we'd ever worn before. When we stood in front of Mum and Dad and paraded up and down in our new clothes they both looked like they were going to cry.

That night we sat round the table and talked non-stop about school. Everyone seemed excited, but I still felt nervous, especially about the language. But for the first time I felt I had a future. That I could be anything I wanted, maybe even an astronaut. Hussein said he wanted to be a doctor, which is what he always said. Hessam didn't have a clue. He was just excited about starting school.

As we watched TV that night and Mum ran around getting everything ready for the next day, Hussein took me and Hessam aside. He whispered so Mum couldn't hear. 'Let's make a pact,' he said.

'What kind of pact?' I asked.

Hussein looked embarrassed. It was as if he wanted to say this but didn't want us to laugh. Then he seemed to have an idea. He pointed at the TV. 'I want us to stick together,' he said. He looked at Hessam. 'Like the Three Musketeers, okay?'

'We did that when we were coming to the UK and, well, I don't want that to stop. So let's make a pact. We stick together till the end, no matter what, always by each other's side.' He pointed to the TV again. 'Like them.'

Somehow, even though Hessam was only seven, we both seemed to know what Hussein was saying. So we bumped fists and promised. Together to the end.

The next morning we woke to bright sunlight. Hussein was up early, keener than anyone to get to school. He said it was his chance to be normal, to do the things that other kids did. But Mum had other ideas. She fussed round him, checking he had everything he needed. I said I thought she wanted Hussein to go to school. She said she did, but it didn't stop her from worrying. I realised that this was the first time we'd be out of Mum's sight for over a year. Every day since we left Herat had been spent together. No wonder she was stressed.

Mum said she had wanted to make a special breakfast for our first day, but that most of the vouchers had been spent on clothes, so it was bread and cheese as usual. It didn't matter – we told her it was the best breakfast ever, just to make her feel better. 'Think about all the times we hadn't had any breakfast at all,' I said. This was definitely better.

As I ate I could feel my tummy churning. Were we going to miss the bus? How would we know where to get off? Would we find our way around the school building? The others seemed excited, so I kept my questions to myself.

As soon as we'd finished eating we went down with the other families to catch the minibus to take us to school. I thought that some of the others looked a bit nervous too, but the volunteers said it was all fine and it was a friendly school. I didn't know the difference between a friendly school and an unfriendly one – the whole thing was new to me. Even going on a minibus was new. As we sat on the bus I looked around at the other kids. How had they got here? Had their journey been as dangerous as ours? The parents had all gathered by the main entrance to watch us leave on the bus. I caught Mum's eye and she smiled, tears welling up. She seemed really proud. Before he got on Hussein ran and gave her one last hug. 'It's okay, I'll look after them,' I heard him say. Mum laughed. 'It's you I'm worried about!'

We waved goodbye and I could see that Mum was crying properly now. It was important to be brave, but here, sitting on the minibus, I didn't feel brave at all. The churning feeling in my tummy started up again, and I felt like I could finally let my fake smile slip. I didn't think I wanted to go to school at all. In fact, I wanted to run. But there was no way I was going to tell Mum that.

I looked at Hessam and saw that he'd stopped smiling too. Perhaps he felt a bit like I did. Then I looked at Hussein. He looked pretty calm, so maybe it was alright. He had said he'd stick by me, no matter what. I wanted to make sure that he meant it.

'You got my back, bro, right?' I said casually.

Hussein laughed, realising straight away how terrified I was. 'Yes of course,' he said. 'You'll be fine, you fool.'

The first stop was the primary school, and Hessam looked nervous as he got ready to leave us and get off the bus. But I knew he was keen to make friends and see what school was like. There were no hugs, just manly pats on the back like we'd seen in the movies. I watched as my little brother stepped down to the waiting primary school staff. I was relieved to see they looked friendly. 'See you later, bro,' I called after him.

As we got nearer and nearer the secondary school stop I managed to go into tough mode. I could see volunteers waiting for us from the school, and I took a big breath. 'Be good' were Hussein's last words of wisdom as we pulled up outside. Then he laughed. How did he always take everything in his stride?

We were met by some friendly faces, and everyone seemed kind. That made me suspicious. Why did people want to help us so much? Did they want money? A teacher took us through the reception area and into the school, and I stayed on red alert. There was something about this place that put me on edge. There were too many people, and they all seemed to want to help us. I remembered what had happened in the Moscow market.

Once we were inside, as I had been dreading, they wanted to separate me and Hussein. I could feel the panic rising as they took him off to a classroom. This wasn't supposed to happen. We said we'd stick together! He seemed totally calm – excited even. I tried to tell the teacher I didn't want to go anywhere without my brother. She only spoke to me in English, slowed down and gesturing with her hands, and I think she was trying to reassure me. So it seemed I had no choice. As I spoke I watched the teacher who had taken Hussein say something to him and I could see he was smiling. I had to make my own way.

I felt my heart racing and I wondered if Hussein's was too. I hoped not, for his sake. I watched as the door to his classroom opened, and I heard a voice from inside say his name.

The door closed behind him. So now it was my turn. By now I wasn't just a bit nervous. I was in full fight-or-flight mode, heart pounding and battling the feeling of wanting to run away. But I couldn't run – I was being ushered towards my classroom. My only option was to face the challenge just like Hussein had. A rush of adrenaline ran through my body. Even though I knew there wouldn't be anything dangerous behind that door, it was like my body thought there would be.

As the door opened, my eyes darted around the room, looking for potential threats. I needed an escape plan. Even when the kind teacher seemed to be asking me how I was, I thought he must be going to do something bad. I just couldn't wait to get out of there.

At lunchtime, when we all took a break, all I wanted to do was get back to Hussein. 'Where's my brother? Can you take me to my brother?' I asked a volunteer. She seemed to know I was serious and took me to find Hussein. We had to go through a maze of rooms and doors and eventually we came to a little office area. Hussein was waiting for me, and I rushed up to him, the anger finally leaving my body.

'What's happened?' he asked.

'This place, bro! It gives me the creeps. Why are they so nice? What do they want?' I realised I sounded like a lunatic.

Hussein seemed to understand. 'Look, this is a chance for us to start over. They're not like the people we've met, you've got to give them a chance.' He took me over to the window and spoke in a whisper. 'We promised to stick together right?'

'I know,' I hissed, 'but you didn't see the way they looked at me!'

Hussein laughed. 'Look, they've been so kind to us,' he said. 'Don't overthink it. Be thankful.'

Hussein smiled. He knew I was just spooked by everyone being so kind. Gradually his presence helped me to calm down. We'd been through such a lot together, he and I, and if I could trust anyone it was my big brother. He said we'd better go then, as it was time for our next class.

'I'm not sure where we are,' I said.

He shrugged. 'Neither am I.'

When we eventually found our next classes and went our separate ways, something kept going through my mind. Hussein had said we had to be grateful. This had annoyed me – Mum and Dad had been through so much and tried so hard to get us here, it hadn't been handed to us on a plate. But then I realised he didn't mean that. He meant his illness. We should be grateful that we could go to school at all. Here was Hussein, in his uniform and starting his classes, but there was a possibility that he wouldn't be able to stay until the end of term. I'd forgotten how delicate his health was right now, and that Mum and Dad were trying to get him to see a specialist. If they wanted to operate, he'd be too sick to stay in school. I decided to stay positive.

Finally the school day was over and I was reunited with Hussein and Hessam back in the minibus. 'Homewards!'

shouted Hussein. I still hadn't got used to the word 'home' – it felt weird to call it that after all this time.

When we got back to the apartment Mum and Dad were waiting for us. Mum hugged us and said she'd felt lost without us and I realised that we'd spent every minute of the day with each other for the past year. Maybe that was why I'd found school so hard too. Dad said it had been a nightmare to keep Mum's mind off it.

I didn't tell Mum and Dad how I really felt that day and Hussein didn't either. We just told them all about our days – about the new equipment we'd never seen before, the teachers and the other kids. What happened at lunchtime would be just between me and Hussein.

I think there was a lot of pretending during those first few weeks. I pretended I was ok at school so as not to worry Mum and Dad, but really I was struggling. I wasn't coping well with the language barrier, and found it really hard to communicate with anyone other than the volunteer translators. I could tell Mum and Dad were keeping something from us too. Every time we asked about Hussein's treatment and when he'd be seeing a doctor, they said it was all in hand. But I could tell how stressed they were. The phone calls they were making were getting nowhere. Why couldn't a specialist make time for Hussein? Mum and Dad said they'd be waiting for him at the hospital. I started to realise that when Mum and Dad had told us there were doctors here they hadn't told the full truth. Did they do it to protect Hussein or because they wanted to believe it themselves?

Then one day, we got home from school and Mum was there waiting for us as usual outside the apartments. Just as we started to walk inside to the apartment, one of the volunteers waved Mum over. Hussein and Hessam and I kicked around for a bit while they chatted, and when Mum came back to us she looked excited. But she wouldn't tell us what had happened. She said we needed to go upstairs and find Dad.

When we got to the apartment Mum rushed us all in. I could see she was shaking, and she wouldn't even wait until we'd put our schoolbags down before she told us.

'We've managed to get an appointment for Hussein at the hospital,' she said. 'With a heart specialist.' She waited, beaming. Dad was speechless. I looked at Hussein. This was the news we'd all been waiting for. Finally, someone would help us to make him better. Dad said it made everything we'd been through to get to the UK worth it. I hoped so.

# CHAPTER 19

# The hospital waiting room

We had a few weeks to wait for the appointment. In the meantime, the main problem was that Hussein refused to tell anyone at school about his illness. He said he didn't want to be any different from the other kids. He wanted to be seen as normal. But I knew that at some point people were going to find out something was wrong. It turned out we didn't have long to wait.

One evening Hussein was restless. Something was worrying him, so I asked him what was up. He took me into our bedroom and showed me his timetable for the next day. PE.

'How am I supposed to do PE without having some kind of episode?' he asked. 'If I do, everyone will know there's something wrong. They'll think I'm a weirdo.'

'You'll be fine,' I said, but even I didn't believe myself. I remembered our football games back in the alleyway in

Herat and how I would watch Hussein, always playing behind him so I could check he was okay. He was much weaker now.

The next day Hussein didn't say anything at breakfast. The minibus picked us up and there were the usual jokes between the three of us. I still wasn't enjoying school and Hussein was still looking after me. I think he quite liked it.

Because our timetables were the same for PE, I'd be doing the lesson with Hussein. It was football. I couldn't wait – I loved football and, anyway, it would be a break from the intensive English classes we had to take. Trying to speak a different language all the time was tiring, and at least in PE no one had to talk much. Football was the same in any language.

As soon as I saw Hussein at the beginning of the class I could tell he was still worried. I also knew he was desperate to fit in with the other boys. We were already different to the others because of where we'd come from and how we spoke. He didn't want to add a heart condition into that. The one thing that Hussein worried about was having to make a big deal of his illness. He'd always tried to play it down. He knew what it meant and what he couldn't do, but he refused to make it who he was.

As we warmed up on the field I looked over at Hussein. He'd gone over to one of the teachers and was saying something to him. I was relieved – he must finally be explaining what was wrong. A volunteer who worked with us was with them too – he knew Hussein's English wasn't that great.

After a few minutes Hussein left the field and went into the changing rooms. The volunteer came over to me.

'Hopefully everything makes sense now,' I said. He smiled but looked puzzled.

'Hussein's just not feeling very well,' he said. 'What do you mean?'

'Oh.' My heart sank.. 'Is that all he said?'

'Yes,' replied the volunteer. 'He's fine – he just wants to skip the lesson.'

I said okay and walked away. But I was mad. Hussein hadn't told them the truth at all! When was he going to come clean? I wished I could tell the teachers myself, but I knew that if I did Hussein would kill me. I decided to talk to him on the way home.

On the bus, Hussein didn't want to listen. I told him he needed to let the teachers know so they could watch out for him. I wasn't in all his lessons and if anything happened no one would know what to do. He shrugged his shoulders.

'I think my teacher knows there's something up anyway,' he said.

'How?' I asked.

'He told me not to worry and whatever was the matter he was there for me.'

'What does that mean?' I questioned.

'Don't know. I guess it means he's kind.'

'You know you're going to have to tell them at some point, bro,' I said. 'These guys care about you. They want to help you.'

'Yeah, I know. I feel guilty about that. But I just want to be normal for a bit longer. There's going to be a fight ahead for me, isn't there? I can't make my heart behave and there's nothing I can do about this illness, but I can make sure I still have a good life. Anyway, I'm supposed to be looking after *you*.'

After that I changed the subject, chatting on and on about school, the English swear words I'd learnt and the nicknames I gave the teachers. Talking was my way of making Hussein feel that things were normal. But we both knew they weren't.

Back at the apartment Mum was already cooking dinner. We teased each other and annoyed Hessam until Mum called us into the kitchen. She said she had some news.

'The appointment's tomorrow,' she said. I turned to Hussein – he looked nervous. All these months of waiting and here we were – we'd finally get to find out what was wrong. Something told me that things would be different from now on, but I didn't know whether they'd be good different or bad different. I realised that part of me didn't want Hussein to go to the appointment at all. I just wanted things to stay the same. But I knew that couldn't happen.

Hussein thought for a minute, then looked into Mum's eyes. 'Great. Let's do this,' he said.

Mum smiled. 'That's my boy.'

I knew Hussein well enough to know that he was putting on a brave face. But that was what Hussein did. No matter what the news or what he had to face, he was always calm. These days, it made him a good big brother to have.

The next morning I could tell that Hussein hadn't slept much. He was already up when I got out of bed, and I started to put my ordinary clothes on. Mum came into the bedroom.

'Hamed, Hessam, it's time for school.' She looked us up and down. 'Why haven't you got your uniforms on?'

'You don't think we're going to school, do you?' I said. 'We're the three musketeers. We stick together.' The three of us bumped fists. Mum sighed. She said something about picking her battles and went back into the kitchen.

The hospital wasn't too far from the apartment, but the journey felt like hours. One of the volunteers came with us to help translate, and I could tell that even he was nervous. The hospital was a big white building just like I'd seen in films, and I could see ambulances coming and going near the front entrance. We had to park a little way away and walk to reception, then follow a maze of corridors to find where we were supposed to be. I couldn't believe how big the hospital was – how did the people working here remember their way around? As we approached the waiting room on the third floor I noticed Hessam had put his hand in Hussein's. We really were going to stick together.

Once we were in the right area of the hospital there was more waiting, but eventually it was Hussein's turn. Mum said we had to stay in the waiting room while they went in with him, so Hessam and I settled down for some more waiting. I almost wished I'd gone to school.

When they finally came out it was just Mum and Dad. Dad said Hussein had gone for a test called an ECG and then he had to have a heart echo. Through the translator they'd managed to tell the cardiologist, Dr Masani, about Hussein's birth, the complicated set of heart problems he'd been born with and the operations he'd had when he was lit- tle. The doctor explained that the racing heart rate was called arrhythmia, and this and the blackouts meant that Hussein's growing body wasn't coping with his heart's problems, and he wanted to find out more about what was going on.

Dad said we'd have to wait a few weeks and then come back to talk about the results. A few weeks? Why couldn't they fix Hussein now? I couldn't work out why it had to take so long. Mum explained that at the moment the doctors had more questions than answers, and they would need to do a lot of tests on Hussein to find out what to do. Worse, because his heart was still growing they might have to wait before they could fix it.

The next two months were like living in a loop. Hussein would go to the hospital for tests, we'd wait a few weeks for the results, then he'd go back to talk to the doctor. Usually that meant going for more tests, with the same thing happening each time. Hussein was off school a lot with all the appointments, and eventually Mum said we needed to tell them.

'No,' protested Hussein. 'They don't need to know! Just tell them I've got a tummy bug again.' But Mum wouldn't listen.

'They know something's wrong, Hussein. They've seen your scars. And you're missing too much school. It's only fair to tell them.'

Hussein looked like he was going to cry with frustration. I was the only one who got it. He'd been hiding it well for months, playing in goal instead of running around the football pitch, choosing cricket teams so he could bowl instead of field. He didn't want to be the boy who was always poorly. That wasn't what he was about.

Eventually, the day came for Mum and Dad to go into school and speak to the teachers. It turned out Hussein hadn't needed to worry. The teachers were brilliant, making sure he could do as much as possible and not treating him any differently. Even Hussein admitted he'd wished we'd come clean sooner.

I couldn't believe the effort the school and hospital went to to give Hussein what he needed. And not just Hussein – all of us. We were treated like royalty, and I couldn't believe we'd ever been ashamed to call ourselves refugees. Mum said we belonged here now.

While Hussein hated missing school, it was obvious to all of us that he was getting weaker. Dad said that as Hussein was getting older his heart was growing too. But one side of his heart was working harder than the other, it was getting bigger, like a muscle. That meant the two sides didn't pump the same, and the doctors needed to work out what to do about it.

I didn't understand exactly what was wrong, but I remember Hussein explaining it to Hessam one day. He held his hand flat like the doctor had done, and described what a valve was and why his wouldn't close properly. 'He'd make a good doctor,' I thought.

At the latest visit to the hospital the doctors had given Hussein a drug that would calm his heart's rhythm. But although it helped with reducing his blackouts, which had become more regular recently, the drug made Hussein sick. His skin went a funny blue colour and Mum said his liver wasn't working well. His eyesight was also getting worse. When Hussein had one of his episodes, the doctors would pump this drug straight into his blood. That made him feel awful, but I guess it saved his life a few times.

As time went on, the drug Hussein took and the way his heart was pumping made it even harder for him to keep up with us. Hessam, always the little one who whinged and moaned, was becoming strong and sporty. It was Hussein who was getting left behind now.

He was now exempt from PE, but he still had to manage the stairs and the trip to school, and over time I realised that even this was a struggle for him. It was easy to forget how frail he was, because he never complained. But one thing was for sure: although his real heart was failing, his other heart – the one that loved people and made him brave – seemed to be stronger than ever. He juggled his hospital appointments and school, catching up where he missed lessons. Whenever I asked him if he minded it all – the appointments, the waiting, the machines and the tests – he always said we were better off than some of the people we'd met on our journey to the UK. He said to think of the people who never made it here at all, the people who weren't so lucky. He told me to imagine what it would be like if we were still in Afghanistan.

All the time Hussein was spending in the hospital seemed to be rubbing off on him. He always seemed to be looking for a way to help people. Then one night as we lay in bed, Hessam sleeping next to us, he said he wanted to tell me about something. 'You'll think I'm weird,' he said, 'but it's changed my life.'

He had been sitting in the waiting room at the hospital, when an old lady came and sat next to him. He said he could tell she was kind by 'the way she smelt'. I teased him forever about this, but secretly I knew what he meant. He said she had seemed anxious, as if it was her first time there, and she asked him if he was waiting for his parents. He realised that he was the youngest person in the room.

'I wanted to help her, bro,' he said.

'I realised that, although I can't run around and do the same things as other people any more, there's still lots I *can* do. I can show people how to be positive.'

He was right. If Hussein had a skill, it was positivity. All those times on our journey when I'd felt like giving up, he was the one who kept me going. It used to help me to think that if he could do it, anyone can. Looking on the bright side was his greatest talent.

'I told her about our journey here,' he said. 'She asked me how I did it – how I stayed happy when things were so tough. So I told her.'

'How *do* you do it?' I asked.

He thought. 'Well, when someone's going through a tough time, you have to hold on to any bit of hope there is. I don't mean saying that everything's going to be okay when it's not – that's just a lie. It's about knowing that things aren't good but being happy with them anyway. That's what you have to do.'

I didn't really get it. I was a natural worrier, and although I pretended I was okay I found it hard to be positive. Hussein shrugged. 'All I know is that I made this old lady feel better, just by talking to her. It felt kind of good.' Then he said that that was what he was going to do from now on – make people feel better. It would be his life's mission. I punched him gently on the arm, and thought how lucky that old lady had been to meet Hussein.

# CHAPTER 20

# Fourteen hours

After the conversation with the old lady, something seemed to change in Hussein. He really did seem to have a new focus – helping other people. It became his job. Even though he was struggling with the side effects of his medication, and he still had the occasional bad episode where his heart rate would skyrocket, he concentrated on doing everything he could for other people.

It was an odd thought, but I started to think that perhaps we'd been brought here for a reason. We nearly didn't make it to the UK. Was it luck that had allowed us to? Or something else? I didn't know if I believed in fate, but I did know that Hussein was a pretty special brother.

The day after Hussein told me about the old lady in the hospital was a Saturday, and we'd been in Cardiff for a few months. The volunteers were rushing around, making preparations for a new batch of refugees who'd be arriving at lunchtime. I couldn't believe how much work went into it. Not long ago this had been happening for us.

We were all quite excited. New refugees meant new people to play with, and we were always looking for kids our own age. We watched out of the window every hour to see if the minibus was arriving. Finally it did. Inside the bus I could see a couple of families, their eyes glued to their new surroundings. I realised we must have looked just as scared.

Hussein said he wanted to go out and talk to them, to tell them it would all be alright. I agreed it would be nice, but then I realised that he was serious. He wanted to be a welcoming committee!

'C'mon bro, let's meet our new friends,' he grinned, and pulled me towards the door. We went downstairs and out into the courtyard. The families were hanging around, probably waiting to be told what to do next. I was a bit embarrassed, but Hussein went straight up to them and started to chat in broken English.

As Hussein prattled on I noticed that the group was mostly looking at him in silence. I tugged at his arm. 'Let's go,' I whispered. He pushed me away. I could have walked away by myself of course, but there was something about Hussein that made me always tag along. When the volunteers came to show people to their accommodation, Hussein made me help with their bags.

After that day Hussein started regularly helping the volunteers with new refugees whenever he could. At first it was simple tasks like translating, as unlike Hessam and me, he'd finally picked up a good level of English. Then as time went on he also helped with the little kids, making sure they felt at home and keeping them occupied while their parents sorted their stuff. He was like everyone's big brother now, not just mine. When a local programme for fixing bikes started, Hussein got his hands dirty and even got some of the kids riding. I wanted to tell everyone that Hussein was secretly fighting his own battle, that everything he did made him tired and weak. But I knew he'd kill me if I did that. He just wanted two things: to be normal and to help.

It always annoyed me that people didn't seem to appreciate what Hussein did. He just got on with it, day after day, helping people in any way he could, but no one seemed to notice the lengths he went to. Then one day, three years since we had first arrived in Cardiff, Mum told us that Hussein was going to win an award. 'You're looking at Volunteer of the Year 2004,' she said proudly. I was proud too! Finally, people knew how big Hussein's real heart was. He got a silver trophy for the award, and Mum put it on the mantel piece in the apartment. Hussein said he didn't care about the trophy too much, but he was glad Mum and Dad were proud.

In between school and the things that kept him busy with our neighbours, Hussein was still spending a lot of time in hospital. The worst times were when the arrhythmia in his heart would get out of control, and we had to rush to the hospital because his heart rate wouldn't regulate. They had to shock him, placing pads either side of his chest before resetting his heart. Each time they did this I thought he was going to die.

*

Hussein's visits to Dr Masani, the cardiologist at the hospital, continued, and he had more ECGs, more echoes and more medication. Dr Masani had become like a member of the family over the months, and apart from the emergencies, I always quite liked going to see him with Hussein. During this time I noticed Hussein's eyesight was getting worse and worse, and his liver was not functioning as it should. It was powerful medication to calm his heart rhythm, but the side effects were becoming a problem. The doctors just wanted Hussein to be older before they could work out what the best operation would be. Dad said maybe there'd be some new medication before then, but in the meantime we just had to wait.

At school, Hussein started his A levels, but he missed lots of classes because of the hospital visits. The doctors started talking about him having a heart transplant, but when they looked into it Mum and Dad said it was too dangerous. The other option was a pacemaker, which Dr Masani said was like a little electric heart that made your real heart beat properly. The problem was that Hussein needed more than a pacemaker. He needed a new heart valve as well, and a procedure to change the electrical activity in his heart. It would be a huge operation. Hussein said he just wanted to get on with his exams.

Miraculously, Hussein managed to attend school enough to finish his A levels. Not only that, but the grades he got were good enough for university. Graduating with a degree became Hussein's ambition, however long it would take him. I hoped it would come true.

But Dr Masani wasn't so sure that Hussein would ever go to university. On one visit he sat us all down in his office with the charts and diagrams on the wall. I couldn't help but notice that he looked nervous.

'The operation Hussein needs is pretty complicated,' he said to Mum and Dad. 'It carries quite a lot of risk. We also can't do it here in Cardiff.'

'I know,' said Mum. 'But they do it in Southampton.' Dr Masani looked at her, surprised.

'Yes, they do,' he said. 'How do you know that?'

Mum explained that after Hussein had his second operation when he was little they'd taken him to Iran. That was where they told him the operation he needed was only performed in two places in the world: the UK and the US.

'This is why we came to the UK,' she smiled.

Dr Masani looked at Hussein, and he spoke to him as if to a friend, rather than a patient. 'It's a risky operation, Hussein. We can't guarantee its success. It's not just about fitting a pacemaker. They'll try to replace the valve that isn't working, and attempt a MAZE procedure that regulates the heart's electrical patterns. Then they'll do a Fontan Revision, which creates an atrial tunnel. It's four operations in one. It's only been done a handful of times before.'

Mum looked worried. But Hussein grinned. 'At least we don't have to go to Chicago.'

Dr Masani smiled, but Dad looked serious. 'What will happen if they don't do it?' he asked.

Dr Masani looked at him. 'Well, we can keep Hussein on the medication, but the side effects might become too much. His liver won't cope forever. He could deteriorate and then we'd need the operation as an emergency anyway.'

I looked at Hussein. He seemed to be weighing it up.

'You don't need to decide now,' said Dr Masani. 'I suggest you go to see the surgeon in Southampton and discuss the options. He'd like to meet you anyway.'

We all trooped out of Dr Masani's room. As soon as he had explained the risks of the operation, Mum had become stressed. Hussein took me to one side.

'In Southampton,' he said, 'I don't want Mum and Dad to be in the consulting room with me.' He looked awkward, but I nodded. I understood: it was getting too much for them. Hussein was twenty years old now – a young man old enough to speak for himself. He just wanted to spare them the worry.

'Will you come in with me instead, bro?' he asked.

I did a tiny fist bump. 'Of course,' I said. 'Musketeers.'

We went home and prepared for the trip to Southampton. As well as clothes and luggage, it felt like we had to pack up our worries and concerns. The only way we were going to get through this was by taking Hussein's advice – to look on the bright side no matter what happens. I promised myself I'd support Hussein and take some of the burden from Mum and Dad.

It took hours to get to Southampton and we were all quiet in the car. When we got there we were shown to an apartment that the hospital lent out to families like us. Hussein had to fill in some forms, and then we were allowed to meet Dr Haw. He was the only doctor ever to have performed this operation successfully, and he was keen to see Hussein.

Hessam stayed with Mum and Dad in the waiting area while Hussein and I went in to see the doctor. I'd never concentrated so much in my life. My English was quite good by now (although not as good as Hussein's) but there was so much to take in. Dr Haw described exactly what would happen in the operation and the difference it would make to Hussein's arrhythmia. He talked about MAZE procedures and the Fontan Revision. The only thing I remember is that there'd be no more blackouts, as the pacemaker would keep the heart's rhythm on track.

Hussein and I listened and nodded, trying to take everything in. When he'd finished he asked if we had any questions, and I knew Hussein and I were both thinking the same thing. How risky was the operation?

When Dr Haw answered, I was surprised at how honest he was. He was treating us like adults.

'The operation is successful in around 60 per cent of cases,' he said. 'But we won't know how likely it is to work for Hussein until we start operating.'

I was stunned. 'So, 40 out of 100 people having this operation don't make it?' I asked. Dr Haw nodded. I thought how glad I was Mum and Dad weren't in the room.

Hussein didn't say much, he just listened and nodded, taking it all in. When we came out I grabbed him.

'It's only a 60 per cent survival rate, bro,' I said. 'Maybe less for you.'

'I know,' he nodded. 'But what's the alternative? I just get worse? I want a normal life.'

'I get it,' I answered. 'But what do we tell Mum and Dad? If we tell them the risk they'll flip.' We went back to the others.

I wasn't sure how we were going to play this one, but as soon as I saw Mum and Dad's anxious faces in the waiting room I knew. Hussein sat down. Suddenly I realised that he expected me to speak. I was horrified. How could I tell Mum and Dad without also making them aware of the risks? Then I remembered all the times Hussein had helped me out, all the times he'd saved my skin. It was the least I could do. I thought of all the times I'd successfully lied to get out of trouble at school.

I sat down with Mum and Dad. I told them what the operation was, what it would involve. But I didn't tell them it could take up to fourteen hours to complete. I also didn't say a word about the survival rate. And I knew I never could. Hussein was an adult now, and only he could make that decision. Why worry Mum and Dad when they weren't the ones who had to choose?

I felt guilty lying to Mum and Dad. We'd been through so much as a family and never hidden anything from each other before. But since we'd come to the UK they hadn't seemed so confident. They didn't have the strength I'd seen on our journey. They struggled with the language and understanding the doctors. The strain of getting us here, losing all their friends and family and the difference in culture in Cardiff and Herat had taken its toll on them. It was like we were the adults now, looking after and being strong for them.

The next few days were spent waiting for test results and for Hussein to have pre-op checks. We were kept occupied, but not busy, passing the time and waiting for the big day. I didn't want it to happen. What if I lost him? Hussein wasn't just my brother – he was my best friend. We'd been through so much together.

The day of the pre-op came. Hussein and Hessam and I teased each other and joked around as usual, but underneath it all was a feeling of trepidation. Hussein was on the ward and had to go through more checks before the next day's operation. By the time they were all done it was late evening. We all sat beside him. I didn't really know what to say, but even in that situation Hussein was thinking of others. He joked and laughed, and I knew he was trying to put us at ease.

After a while Dr Haw came in with a piece of green paper. He said this was the important bit, the bit where Hussein had to sign his consent to the operation tomorrow morning. He explained that the piece of paper described the risks of the operation and if Hussein signed it he was agreeing to accept those risks.

We were all quiet. I didn't want to say anything – how could anyone tell Hussein what to do when it could only be his decision? If I could I'd have told him not to sign that consent form. I'd have told him to carry on as things were and not to risk his life for something that might not work. After everything Dr Haw had described it felt as if Hussein signed that paper he'd be signing his life away. But I knew I had to keep quiet. No one could make this decision except for Hussein.

Mum seemed to agree. 'Whatever you decide, we're by your side,' she said. I wondered how she'd feel if she knew the odds.

We all tried not to look at that green piece of paper, as if we could ignore it and the operation would go away. But it wasn't going to go away. If Hussein didn't sign the green paper now, his health would continue to deteriorate until he was back here in the operating room anyway. It was the only option.

The only person who didn't seem afraid of that piece of paper was Hussein. He looked around the room and smiled, amused at how tense we all looked. Then he turned to the nurse. 'Well, I'll need a pen,' he grinned. Typical Hussein. I knew he didn't want this op. I knew he was just as scared as we were that it would go wrong. I knew he wanted to stay with us, teasing his brothers and playing the fool. I knew how much he wanted to go to university. But he never took time to dwell on the bad stuff. For Hussein it was all about moving forward. He passed the paper back to Dr Haw. It was like he'd signed an autograph.

'Now we can all go to sleep, people!' he said to the nurses and doctors in the room. They seemed surprised at how relaxed he was about the following day, but we weren't. We knew Hussein, and this was just what he was like.

No one got much sleep that night. Mum cried so much during our morning prayers that at breakfast her cheeks were red and blotchy. Hessam and I knew that we needed to be strong, so we put on a brave face. Dad did too, but his way of dealing with it was to take himself off for a long walk. He always said that if you tire the body, you numb the mind. I found out afterwards that in the early hours of the morning he'd gone to the ward to watch Hussein sleeping.

We didn't eat much breakfast and made our way straight to the hospital. To our surprise, as we got to Hussein's room we could hear laughter coming from inside. I shouldn't have been surprised. Hussein was joking with the other patients and teasing the nurses as they prepared him for the op.

The atmosphere Hussein had created helped. He'd succeeded in lightening the mood. I saw that he'd already got
a theatre gown on but was struggling to tie the knots, and I
burst out laughing when I saw his ass sticking out the back.
Even Mum and Dad smiled, and I was grateful to Hussein for
making this easier for them. Before he went into the operating theatre we all huddled together. There was nothing to
say now, so we all stayed quiet. Then, after a final check, the
nurses told us it was time for Hussein to go. They unplugged
the machines that were attached to him and wheeled him away.

'See you soon, guys!' Hussein shouted to his roommates
as the squeaky wheels of the bed started to turn. We followed
behind, together with some of the nurses. We all knew what
was about to happen but none of us could prepare for it no
matter how hard we tried.

We went down in a lift and then towards the theatre, and
soon we got to a big red sign that said 'no entry'. Here was
where we had to stay. The nurse whispered, 'Time to say
cheerio.' That made Mum break down in tears. None of us
wanted to say that! How could we, knowing that we might not
be able to say hello again? This wasn't a goodbye before a holiday or when someone went off to school. This could be forever.

Dad couldn't say it. He was crying too and wandered off
down the corridor. I was disappointed in him. Was that it?
He wasn't even going to say goodbye to his eldest son? What
if he never saw Hussein again? Hessam and I both went up
to Hussein. 'See you in a few hours,' I said, and shook him by
the hand. It was all I could do to control my emotions. Then
they started to wheel him in. Just before they did, Dad came
back and kissed him on the forehead.

CHAPTER 21

# The prayer room

As soon as they pushed Hussein into the operating theatre and I heard the door click shut my heart took over. I couldn't hold the emotion in any more and I had to get away. I said something about getting a chair for Mum and ran off down the corridor. I instinctively headed towards the waiting room, but as I got nearer I realised I didn't want to be there either. I needed to be on my own.

There was a prayer room on the operating floor and I knew that was where I needed to be. I ran towards it, repeating in my head, 'You will see him again.' I prayed there wouldn't be anyone in there.

There wasn't. Hessam was with Mum, Dad had gone for a walk and Hussein was in the hands of the surgeons, so it was finally just me. I tried to deal with my thoughts. But they were so muddled, all I could do was cry. The tears

streamed down my face. They were for the last few years of
Hussein struggling, the terrifying journey we'd all endured
to get us here, the rollercoaster of emotions as Hussein had
all his tests, and for having to hold it together for so long to
protect Mum and Dad.

The one person who could have comforted me then was
Hussein, but he was the one person who couldn't be there.
I'd never felt so alone.

The tears came and went, and as they stopped I looked
around the room. I wondered how many other people had
knelt here, praying for someone to pull through something?

I didn't want to ask God for anything. I knew I hadn't
been a good person. I'd hurt people, messed around in school,
made the wrong choices. Why should God listen to me
instead of all the other people who needed his help? During
those few hours I begged and pleaded with God. I promised
anything – I'd be a better person, help people like Hussein,
swear less – anything if he would just give me one thing.
My brother. As the hours passed, I thought of more promises, more things I would do if God could just make it that
Hussein was okay. I'd volunteer like Hussein, help people
who were less fortunate than us, give back to all those who'd
helped me settle in in the UK. Anything, just to have my
brother.

After a couple of hours I heard the door to the prayer
room open. My heart sank, but as I looked up I realised that
it was Mum and Hessam, come to do some bargaining of
their own. Mum was crying so much she could barely get up
off the floor from her prayers. I whispered to Hessam, asking
him where Dad was. He whispered back that he was doing

laps of the hospital. 'The construction workers have even got to know him,' he smiled.

We left Mum in the prayer room and went out into the corridor. Finding ourselves back where we started, by the doors they took Hussein through, we found Dad. They'd been operating for nearly five hours.

Dad wanted to know if there was any news, but we'd already buzzed to ask and been told that they'd let us know soon. But as the hours went by it became harder and harder to bear.

Ten hours in, and still there was no news. I went back to the prayer room, where I found Mum being comforted by a nurse. I realised it didn't matter what religion you were in situations like these.

After twelve hours I was convinced there had been complications. I buzzed again and again, but this time the nurses didn't respond. I rested my head on the door. 'Please God,' I whispered. 'I promised him I'd always be there.'

It was like someone heard my prayer, because as soon as I'd said it a voice came over the telecom system. 'We'll be out with an update shortly,' it said.

What did that mean? Was it good news? Or were they going to tell us something terrible? Hessam had heard the buzzer and rushed towards me. I motioned to him not to disturb Mum. 'I don't want her to come out until they've got something to tell us,' I said.

We waited by the metal door, looking up and down the corridor to check that Mum and Dad weren't around. Then there was a faint 'beep', and I could hear the inner doors opening and closing. I held my breath.

The metal outer door unlocked and Dr Haw came out. His face was hidden behind a surgical mask, so it was difficult to read his expression. Hessam and I said nothing, both of us afraid to ask. Dr Haw slowly removed his mask.

'The surgery was a success,' he smiled. 'We're really pleased with how Hussein is doing.'

I broke down in tears. Hessam hugged Dr Haw – to the surprise of both of them – and we started to repeat 'Thank you, thank you' over and over.

Dr Haw explained that he needed to get back to the theatre now as the finishing up was still in progress. We let him go, but not without thanking him one more time. Then Hessam went outside to find Dad and I headed to the prayer room to tell Mum the good news.

The operation had taken fourteen hours and 32 minutes. Hussein was semi-conscious now and doing well on the coronary care unit (CCU) ward. The nurses told us that two people could go in and say hello.

There was no stopping Mum, but Dad was hesitant. He could never bear seeing any of us cut or bleeding, and I knew he didn't want to see his son in that condition. I remembered the night Dad had been captured by the Taliban. I thought he was the bravest person in the world then. When it came to his children it was different.

I said I'd go with Mum, so we waited to be buzzed in by the nurse. We walked through a dark corridor before coming out in front of another set of doors. I guessed all this security was to prevent infection.

As the doors opened and we went into the CCU, all I could see were machines and wires. Then I saw Hussein. He was still drowsy from the anaesthetic and he was linked up to lots of screens and buttons. He looked small among all the machinery.

'He looks in so much pain,' Mum said in a hoarse voice. 'Why are there still so many tubes?'

The nurse said the tubes were necessary – they had to drain off the fluid from Hussein's chest. It was very important after such complicated open-heart surgery.

All I could focus on was that Hussein was alive. He looked frail and his eyes were barely open, but he was there and I could look into his face and see that he recognised me. I didn't say anything, but it was like he could read my thoughts anyway. I'd promised I'd be there and now I was.

None of us had been able to eat for the last fourteen hours, and the stress of seeing her son in this situation, connected to so many tubes and monitors, was too much for Mum. Suddenly I felt her lean against me and I realised she was losing consciousness. I could see she was trying her hardest to keep her head straight, but the blackness was closing in. I grabbed onto her and pulled her away from Hussein. She tried to resist but she was so limp that I was able to bring her towards the exit doors. The doors opened, and Dad was standing on the other side of them. I called for Hessam to fetch a chair for Mum (a real one this time) and he ran and got one.

But I was desperate to get back to Hussein. As I turned to go back into the CCU room Dad stopped me and said he wanted to come with me, so together we went back in. He was also shocked by all the tubes and machines, but then Hussein gave him a little nod and I could see that Dad was finally relaxing.

But then he whispered how hot it was, and I realised that he, too, was about to pass out. I grabbed hold of him and held him firmly as I felt his legs give way.

I gently guided him towards the door too, and when it opened I told Hessam that we needed another chair. The nurses must have seen this reaction a lot, as they went to get some water for Mum and Dad. Mum said she could feel the sensation coming back to her fingers.

With a jolt she asked, 'Who's with Hussein?' I held her hands.

'It's ok, he's resting now. We need to let him sleep.'

'Go in, will you Hamed?' she said. 'I want him to know there's someone there.'

So I went back into the ward. Hussein seemed more awake now, and he looked at me and said in a frail voice: 'Where's Mum?'

'She's fine,' I stumbled. 'They had to go to pray.'

Hussein smiled, and I knew he was laughing at me for making up such a rubbish lie. Then he closed his eyes and fell asleep.

I knew there would be a long road to recovery ahead of us. But I also knew that Hussein was through the worst of it. And that I wouldn't be leaving his side any time soon.

# CHAPTER 22

# Recovery

O ver the next few days we tried to focus on the success of the operation and what Hussein had to do to get well. But he still looked frail – his ribcage had been broken during the operation so it was hard for him to talk or laugh – and he had an alarming scar running all the way down his chest. We spent every possible minute with him there in the CCU and I longed to tease and laugh with him, but Mum told us to keep the jokes to a minimum.

The nurses in the CCU were amazing, and within a few days they said Hussein could go back onto the cardiology ward. As they wheeled him up there, a neatly folded towel placed over his scar, everyone on the ward cheered. Hussein held the towel in place with one hand and raised the other in a thumbs up. He was like a returning champion.

Dad was happy to have his rubbish joke partner back again, and Mum was so relieved that her oldest 'baby' was going to be okay. I just couldn't wait for Hussein to get out of hospital so we could start our night time chats again.

Even though we were all keen to get home, Southampton had become like a second home for us by now. We'd spent so much time with the nurses and doctors there, and the other patients, that they were starting to feel like family. Dad couldn't believe the level of care we were shown, given that we weren't even from the UK. Mum said after all we'd been through Hussein deserved the best.

Because of how rare the operation Hussein had received was, he was the focus of a lot of attention. Doctor after doctor came to meet him and chat to Dr Haw about the procedure. On one occasion Hussein pretended he'd had enough. 'Do I look like a case study to you people?' he teased, mock-angrily. The junior doctors looked embarrassed, until Hussein burst out laughing and told them he was just kidding.

Each night the nurses had to physically kick us out as none of us wanted to leave Hussein on his own. He said he didn't mind, but he told me afterwards that he found those nights quite hard. The nurses cared for him brilliantly, but the hardest thing was being alone with his thoughts. He told me one day that he was feeling stronger than before the operation, and that he had a purpose now, and that purpose was to help people. He said he'd had a lucky escape, and the least he could do was to pay that forward to people in need. I could tell he was itching to get out of hospital so he could make a start.

One day I looked at his long scar, bright red on his chest.

'I wonder what's going on under there,' I said.

'Same thing that's going on under yours hopefully,' he grinned. He patted his chest. 'It's good as new, this.' But we both knew we could hear the opening and closing of the new metallic valve, keeping his heart beating steadily. We also knew that some of his right ventricle had been removed to take the pressure off. So he had less heart than he'd had before. I thought it was more like the other way around – everything that happened to Hussein seemed to make his heart grow.

Before long Hussein was able to take his first steps. The nurses cheered him on as he walked one, then two paces across the ward. He was getting stronger every day, and soon we'd be able to leave hospital and go back to normal. That word always felt funny for our family, as ever since that night where we had to hide on the roof to escape the Taliban there hadn't been any such thing. There was no normal for us.

Eventually the day came for us to leave Southampton. There were tears from the nurses as they waved us off, and I knew that Hussein had been a very special patient for them. We had been living there for over two months while Hussein recovered, and it felt like the last day of a holiday, or leaving extended family. They'd never once referred to the fact that we'd been refugees just a short time ago. They treated Hussein like he was the most important person on earth, and they were so proud to hear of all his future plans. We were forever indebted to the staff at Southampton, and all of us would miss them.

The journey back to Cardiff was a long one, but not as long as the journey Hussein had in front of him. He was still saying he was determined to go to university, but Mum said he had some work to do first. For a start, he'd have to get back to his studies.

Slowly but surely Hussein got stronger over the next few months. He gained more energy, and as his ribcage healed he was able to laugh properly again. Our night time chats were back, and we passed the hours before we fell asleep talking about all sorts of random topics. Sometimes we'd joke; sometimes it would end in an argument. But I could always confide in Hussein without the fear that he would tell Mum and Dad. Often, I'd make things up just because I wanted to talk to him. I was so glad to have my big brother back.

Although everyone knew how patient Hussein was, the one thing he was impatient about was getting back to his studies. Mum and Dad weren't sure whether he was strong enough for university, but Hussein said he could study at the nearby University of South Wales (USW) and still live at home. He was determined. I understood why Mum and Dad didn't want him to go, but I also knew that Hussein was an adult now, and he would always do what he wanted anyway. So he started his application.

While Hussein was planning for university, academically, I wasn't doing so well. I'd missed lots of lessons while Hussein was having his operation and only managed to scrape five GCSEs. Now it was time to do A levels, and I knew Mum and Dad had high expectations for me. But I was out of my depth. I couldn't shake off the fact that getting to the UK had always seemed like a dream. I couldn't face the reality of us living here, never mind of school and university. But there were no more excuses. I couldn't use the fact that we were refugees, or that my face didn't fit – all that was years behind us now. I had to accept that I was a failure.

One night, when we were in our beds, I couldn't stop worrying.

'What are you plotting?' Hussein asked when he noticed how quiet I was.

'Nothing. I'm just worried about school.'

'How come?'

I explained that I was struggling with A levels and didn't think I'd ever make it to university like him. I didn't want that to happen, but my main worry was that Mum and Dad would think I was a failure.

'They made so many sacrifices,' I said.

We talked for hours then, me pouring my heart out to my bigger, braver, wiser brother about everything I thought I couldn't achieve. We discussed what other options I had, or which subjects I could choose. Eventually – as I knew he would – Hussein came up with a plan. I would sit a community language A level in Farsi alongside my other exams. It would give me more qualifications and help me with my confidence. By late into the night I'd started to smile again.

Eventually a day came for Hussein that none of us ever thought would happen: his first day at university. As usual Hussein took it in his stride, and if you asked him he would always say that he was meant to be there. Through everything he'd always had an unshakeable faith – that he was here for a reason.

Looking around the campus that day, at all the people

from every corner of the world, it was clear they were gathered for one thing: to follow their dreams and ambitions. I thought back to our journey to get here, hiding in fields at night, being abandoned in jungles and travelling in cramped shipping containers. Hussein was just the same as any other student now, nothing more, nothing less. He'd achieved his ambition.

Hussein took to university life brilliantly. Unlike the other students, he never complained about assignments or exams, and he enjoyed every day. He told me once, that when we complain about a rainy day, we forget that for someone somewhere a rainy day means water for their crops. And some people don't live to see another rainy day at all. We just have to be grateful.

But while Hussein was full of optimism, I was dreading every day – rainy or not. My fear of failing my A levels was catching up with me again, and I couldn't bear the disappointment Mum and Dad would feel if I flunked my exams. Whenever they asked me about my studies I would lie, saying everything was 'going well'. But it wasn't. And the worst thing was that I couldn't blame the people around me or my circumstances. Look at Hussein! After everything he'd been through, there he was at university. My life felt like it was slipping out of my control.

Hussein noticed I wasn't myself. I wasn't sleeping well, and our night time chats were becoming more awkward. He'd even try to entice me with a topic he knew would make me argue, but I couldn't be bothered to rise to the bait.

Hussein was coming to the end of his first year at university when I was due to get my A level results. We drove to school together – Mum, Dad, me, Hessam and Hussein, but I told them I wanted to go in by myself. I remember walking slowly into the school building and being greeted by the cheers of students who'd obviously got the results they wanted. I felt sick.

I got to the lower school hall, and the teacher looked through the names in alphabetical order for me. Then he placed an envelope into my hands. It felt like my future was folded up in a piece of paper.

The one thing I'd learnt over the last few years was that you have to face your fears head on. I tore open the envelope. I knew it would be bad, but I hadn't expected it to be that bad. Next to the subjects I'd agonised so much over there were three 'U's.

I felt the blood rush away from my face. Well, I wasn't going to be an astronaut then. My next thought was how I was going to face my teachers and, more importantly, my family waiting outside. How could I tell Hussein that I couldn't even get a single A level?

Most of the other students had left by now, which was good because I was terrified of someone asking me what I got. I knew I couldn't stay here much longer – I had to go out and tell the others.

I walked out to the car, and as I opened the door I sensed something in Mum. We had always shared a sense of intuition, and I wondered if she could tell it was bad news without me even saying a word.

'How did it go?' she asked in a soothing voice. She knew. This was her way of telling that she was proud of me no matter what.

I couldn't bear to do it. Hussein grabbed the paper and looked at it. He showed no expression. Then he said, 'What about the community language result?' Suddenly I remembered. I'd forgotten to pick up the separate results paper! I bolted out of the car and ran back into school. The teacher was still there and he handed me another piece of paper. Surely there was some hope?

There was. I'd passed. It still wasn't great, but at least I had one qualification. I went back to the car, and while I'd been gone Hussein had obviously showed Mum and Dad the three 'U's. Mum seemed a little disappointed but okay, but Dad could hardly look at me. I knew that, even with the community language result, I'd failed them.

Dad stayed silent the whole way home. No words, just a look I'll never forget. I'd let him down and it was all my fault. I felt like a spoilt kid who'd thrown away all the sacrifices his parents had made to get him to a better place. I'd had more opportunities for education than anyone in Herat would ever have, and I'd thrown it down the drain.

Over the next few weeks I closed myself off from my friends and family. I resigned myself to a menial job, and left any dreams I had of a better life back there in school. Even the result of the community language couldn't bring me any hope.

I stopped going out in case I saw someone from school and they asked me about my future plans. Hussein knew I was in a dark place, and he tried to cheer me up and help me to think about what I could do next, but I wasn't listening. I missed our night time chats, but I couldn't bring myself out of the mental state.

'You have to stop punishing yourself,' he'd say. But that was exactly what I wanted to do.

I think Hussein knew that I was starting down a road from which I wouldn't recover unless I got some help. It was his turn to be there for me.

One day he came home from university and took me into the sitting room. He was beaming. 'I've got some good news,' he said. He was so excited he could hardly stand still.

'What is it? Why are you being weird?' I asked.

'USW have agreed to accept you to do the computer science foundation year,' he said. I didn't understand.

'Me? How? I didn't even apply. I don't even have any A levels.' I couldn't work out what he was saying.

'You do – you have your community language. I told them your result and asked them if they'd consider letting you try the foundation year based on that. They took a bit of persuading,' here he grinned, 'but they say given our circumstances as a family they're willing to give you a go.'

I couldn't believe that Hussein had been doing all of this behind the scenes, without my knowledge for the last few weeks. I could just imagine how difficult it would have been for the people at USW to say no to him – no one could ever say no to Hussein – but he must have had a hell of a job convincing them based on one rubbish A level.

'This is probably your last chance though, bro,' he said seriously. 'Don't mess it up.'

There was no chance I was going to do that. Things would be different now – no messing around, no laziness. I was going to work like I'd never worked before. This wasn't about me any more – I absolutely couldn't let Hussein down.

# CHAPTER 23

# Angels in lab coats and overalls

The next year – 2007 – was a good year for our family. Hussein's health was stable, we were both enjoying our university courses, and Hessam was also doing well in his studies. We had been in the UK for six years and we finally felt that things were working out for us.

Mum and Dad's main struggle was with the language. It still wasn't coming easily to them, and we often had to help them with everyday tasks. I passed my foundation year and became a fully fledged student. Family mealtimes felt like they had done years ago – full of laughter, Dad's terrible jokes and Mum telling us all to pipe down. But the main difference was that there was no fear. No fear of the Taliban, no fear of not being able to get to a safe haven, no fear of Hussein's health deteriorating. Things were good.

We decided to take a holiday. There followed weeks and

weeks of discussions about where we would go, often ending with some ridiculous suggestions. But we eventually settled on France. Mum's aunt was living there so we could stay with her, and her husband was one of Dad's best friends, so it would be a reunion for all of us. Dad in particular found it hard to connect with people these days. The language barrier and the effects of our traumatic journey meant that he hadn't made many friends in Cardiff. This holiday would be an opportunity for him to spend some quality time with people he loved.

It was strange to think of returning to France when the last time we were there things were so different. This time we were legal and had nothing to fear, but it still felt wrong to be leaving the UK. I couldn't help feeling that somehow we wouldn't be allowed back in. At border control, it felt good to say we were from the UK. We'd always be Afghan of course, but after everything it had done for us we were proud to call the UK home.

As we left the UK my mind flashed back to hiding in tyres, chasing the train and being caught by the police dog. Now, instead of hiding we could sit proudly on the train, excited about our holiday.

Lyon was just what we needed. It was warm and relaxing, and Mum and Dad loved being with family. I realised how much they'd left behind when we fled Herat. When the holiday came to an end and it was time to say goodbye, Mum cried.

Hussein was eager to get back to university after that summer. He still had a sense that it was a race for him to achieve everything he wanted, as if he didn't have all the time in the world. He was a brilliant student. I would wait for him after lectures to go home together, and more often than not I would have to go and find him, and remind him it was time to leave. One day, angry that he'd made me wait for so long, I went to find him, only to discover that he was deep in conversation in the library with another student – someone who needed some extra help.

It rubbed off on me. I realised that, whether you have eight years or 80, your time is still limited. Hussein hadn't just helped me with my education, he'd helped me to realise that there's no time to waste in chasing your goals. Being positive was a craft, and he was the craftsman.

Although Hussein was well, I knew that his pace of life and everything he threw himself into took its toll on his heart. With a reduced right ventricle and a pacemaker, he still had to be careful. But it was his other heart that was working the hardest. Even though he had so much he wanted to achieve, his first thought was always to see how he could help someone else. In this he was relentless.

In 2009 a day came that none of us had ever thought we'd see. Hussein brought a letter home to Mum and Dad and translated it as they stared at it. He'd be graduating from university with his degree in Network Management and Security in June.

Mum put her hands over her mouth. We all knew what this day meant. Not just that Hussein had completed his degree, but that one of us had succeeded in our new country. It meant that Hussein, who three years ago had been on the operating table in Southampton having one of the most complex heart operations there is, was now a graduate.

I have a photograph of that day that makes me smile. It shows the three of us boys, smart in new suits and with fresh haircuts, standing proudly together. Hessam had polished all our shoes to death, saying they had to be extra shiny, but of course you can't see them in the photo. Hussein has his gown on, and Mum and Dad are either side of us. Dad has a grimace on his face, and I remember how the photographer kept asking us to move closer together. Dad got impatient and kept fidgeting, trying desperately to loosen the tight top button of his new shirt. We couldn't stop laughing. In the end it was all captured on camera – Hussein looking at Dad instead of at the camera and Hessam and me giggling. But nothing could take away from how proud we all were of Hussein.

Sometimes, all you want is to stop time. There is often a moment or event where we look around us and realise we're in that 'sweet spot' – that rare moment where everything seems perfect. Hussein's graduation day was that moment for me. His operation felt like a distant memory and the future felt bright for all of us.

Thanks to Hussein's help, I flew through university. I graduated with a 2:1 in Computer Science and went on to get a job with one of the largest ICT employers in Wales, as an application analyst. After my failures at school I had lost faith in my own ability, but seeing Hussein take himself through university I knew that school wasn't the end, and that there was so much more to come. The drive he gave me is something I'll always be thankful for.

During this time, Hussein's health was stable, and he used his degree to set up an IT consultancy firm with his best friend Moe. The company was doing well, and we all enjoyed riding Hussein's success with him.

But within a few months of the company launching, Hussein started to say that something felt wrong. It started with him being sick during the day. There didn't seem to be a reason for it, and it was happening way too regularly for it to be a bug. He seemed wary, as if his old enemy was rearing its head.

At first the sickness seemed dependent on what Hussein ate. Eggs seemed to be a trigger, but the doctors tested for an allergy and found nothing. One of the frustrating things about Hussein's condition was the doctors' lack of knowledge. It wasn't their fault – they had nothing to compare it to, and because he had several rare conditions, he was always uncharted waters.

Hussein was making more and more visits to the doctor, and we all knew this wasn't a good sign. Perhaps it was stomach acid? Reflux? A reaction to some unknown chemical?

He started to hide his sickness, throwing up in secret and refusing to tell Mum and Dad, getting Hessam and me to cover for him. As Mum and Dad got older we all felt it was our duty to protect them, but Hussein had always taken this very seriously. Ever since we'd arrived in the UK he'd told me how much they'd sacrificed to get us here and how much they'd gone through. 'Don't let us be a burden,' he'd say.

Time passed, and Hessam too started university. One day I was at work Mum's name came up on my phone. 'Hey, Mum,' I answered, surprised. Then something in my stomach lurched. She was sobbing.

'It's Hussein. *Megan tamoom karedeh.*'

I stopped dead. Her words in Farsi meant 'They are saying he is done.' What did that mean? I went straight to my manager and told him I needed to leave for the hospital straight away. I couldn't stop hearing Mum's words in my head. I rushed to my car.

On the way to the car park I tried calling Mum back, but she didn't answer. I just wanted to speak to her and find out what was going on. Why wouldn't she pick up the phone? I swore as I turned out of the car park and headed for the motorway. There was traffic, and I begged silently for drivers in front to move out of the way.

My mouth was dry and I realised I was holding my breath. Ever since we travelled as stowaways in the lorry this was something I'd do when I was under stress. I screeched into the hospital car park and dumped the car by the barrier. Running up the stairs to the cardiology department I knew so well, I was terrified of what I would find. Although I was desperate to see if Hussein was okay, I could also hear his words echoing in my mind: 'Don't be a burden.' Hussein would want me to protect Mum and Dad from whatever was happening. I knew I couldn't break this promise.

I heard Mum before I saw her. Her crying was echoing down the corridor and I panicked that I was already too late. I pushed my fear down – deep inside me like I'd done on so many other occasions – and ran towards Mum.

She fell into my arms and said that Hussein was with the cardiologist. She didn't know what was going on, they hadn't told them anything and he had been in there for a while. She pointed to the door that led to the ward.

'Let me go and find out, Mum,' I said. I was itching to get behind that door, where I knew my precious brother was in some sort of serious trouble. But my legs were heavy. I put my face to the circular glass of the door's window, hoping to be able to prepare myself for what was to come. I could see the nurses' station. It was deserted. In fact, there was no one around at all. At the end of the room was another set of doors with a similar small window in it. Behind it I could see people milling about. So that was where all the commotion was.

Suddenly a nurse rushed out of that door and bent to prop it open. She ran to fetch some medical equipment and wheeled it back through into the room. Behind her I could see Hussein, the pads on his chest, lying motionless on a trolley. They were shocking him again.

I wished that what I was seeing wasn't real. But my face stayed pressed up against that little circle of glass, fixing my eyes on Hussein. Then the nurse came and closed the door, blocking my view. I suddenly remembered that Mum was behind me, desperately waiting for some news. What could I tell her?

I hated lying. But I didn't have any choice. I needed to give God a chance to bring my brother back.

'They are still working on him, Mum' was the best I could do.

The wait was becoming unbearable. It was just like Hussein's big op, except at least then the doctors were fixing something that was in their control. Right now it was as if they were fighting against time.

Eventually the door opened again and I stepped back. The doctor was coming. I braced myself, knowing that I had to somehow keep Mum calm. I tried to read this doctor's body language, and I noticed that he was avoiding eye contact. This didn't feel good.

I knew this doctor, and he was normally one of the chatty ones, treating us more like friends than relations of a patient. I knew that his silence wasn't a good sign. He sat us down.

'There have been some complications with Hussein's pacemaker. We don't know why, but it's become ineffective. It's highly unusual in such a short space of time. The arrhythmia has therefore caused a lot of problems for Hussein. We had to shock him to restart his heart.' I could see he was clenching his jaw. Mum was shaking. 'Is he okay?'

'He's as stable as we can get him,' nodded the doctor. 'But this raises bigger questions about what we'll have to do now. At the moment, I don't know the solution. It might mean another op. But we know that's not straightforward.'

I looked at Mum. We both knew that Hussein's pacemaker had been placed in his belly rather than next to his heart, which was unusual, so another operation would be incredibly risky.

'So what happens now?' I asked.

'We're prepping him for theatre so we can take a look at what's going on,' said the doctor. 'But in the meantime we're also waiting on a call from Southampton and some cardiology experts at University Hospital Bristol.'

After that the waiting was unbearable. Dad and Hessam arrived and we all sat in the private waiting room as the doctors discussed what to do. They didn't want to operate on Hussein unless they had to, but they didn't have much time to wait for advice. For whatever reason, Hussein's pacemaker wasn't working. This meant he was relying on his own heart to keep him alive – something it couldn't do for long.

After a few hours, Dr Masani came to see us. He seemed agitated.

'We've had a call from University Hospital Bristol and I've spoken to the cardiologist there. They've got a different theory – quite a surprising one. They don't think the problem is a faulty pacemaker at all, but rather that something's interfering with how the pacemaker is working. They think that could be Hussein's medication. There isn't much research to support it, but then there isn't much research on cases like Hussein's anyway. They think a chemical in the medication is corroding the pacemaker.'

Dr Masani waited patiently as I explained what he'd just said to Mum and Dad in Farsi. But I didn't really understand it myself. How could Hussein's medication be doing more harm than good? There wasn't time to argue. If Bristol were right, draining the medication from Hussein's circulation system might solve the problem. The dilemma was, how long could we wait to find out if this was the case?

Dr Masani left us, and once again we were alone in the waiting room. We didn't know whether Hussein would be having a dangerous operation any minute or whether this untested theory could save him in the nick of time. What if they waited to test this theory and it turned out to be wrong? All we could do was pray and leave it in the hands of the doctors.

After another hour or so Dr Masani came back. He said that Bristol were so confident in their theory that they'd decided to go with it. They'd agreed for Hussein to be transferred as an emergency to Bristol while they tried to formalise their theory. Once he got there, they'd try to drain the medication from his body and restart the pacemaker.

We followed the ambulance with its blazing blue lights all the way to Bristol. On the way I kept thinking that the only thing that was waiting for us at that hospital was hope. We just had to get there in time. I didn't take my eyes off that ambulance the whole journey.

When we got to the hospital, Hussein was rushed into the cardiology unit and we followed behind. The doctors were on hand with fluids ready to flush out the medication from his system. They just had to hope that the pacemaker wasn't too damaged to be restarted.

When we got to the CCU we were once again left behind as they rushed Hussein behind closed doors. Although we were used to being kept away by now, it didn't get any easier. Dad went back to his pacing, busying his body so he could control his mind. Mum prayed quietly, and I remembered Hussein's instructions. I had to look after them. I wouldn't let him down.

As time went on I started to worry that we'd have another fourteen-hour wait like the last time. But after just a few hours a doctor came through to tell us that they'd tested the theory and were confident it would work. They would go ahead and drain Hussein's body of the medication.

I felt like I was holding my breath. Would the pacemaker be good enough to restart? It was the only thing keeping Hussein alive.

It was only a couple of hours later that the Bristol doctor came out to see us. I stood up as he came back through the double doors. He took off his mask.

'It's worked,' he smiled. Mum ran to him and hugged him. 'We've managed to restart the pacemaker and regulate the rhythm of Hussein's heart. As it kicks in he should regain consciousness.'

The doctor was right. Over the next few hours Hussein gradually came round – to a sea of faces he didn't recognise. He joked afterwards that he thought he was on the other side and was surrounded by angels, except these ones were in lab coats and blue overalls. He was dazed, but I knew his old self was returning when he started to play up with the doctors. Unused to his sense of humour, the doctors explained how unpredictable the situation had been.

'You were in a pretty dangerous spot at one point,' one of them said.

'That's okay,' Hussein said. 'Danger's my middle name.'

We spent the next few days at Bristol while Hussein recovered. He couldn't care less that he'd had another close call. He was only in awe of the level of care the doctors and nurses of yet another hospital were giving him. Although he knew now they weren't angels, he told me they might as well be, as they sat by his bed and cared for him long after they had to. Whether in Cardiff, Bristol or Southampton, it seemed wherever Hussein's heart took him, he found kindness and compassion.

Seeing the kindness of strangers was good for me, too. I still struggled with accepting help from people I didn't know, my first thought at an offer of help was always 'What's in it for them?' Over those few days in Bristol, Hussein taught me to accept that kindness had existed all along.

While the safe haven of the UK gave us stability, it was the NHS that had saved Hussein's life. And during that time in Bristol he confided in me again that he felt he had a purpose. This time he didn't just want to help random strangers. He wanted to give back to the NHS everything they'd given to him.

# CHAPTER 24

# An extraordinary life

As Hussein recovered at Bristol, we all spent a lot of time at the hospital. During the day Hessam and I were mostly in the waiting room, and Hussein would weave back and forth between there and the ward.

One day I was standing with him in the corridor when a man came up to us.

'Excuse me, do you know where the doctor's office is?' he asked. Hussein and I both noticed that he looked anxious. He seemed distant, and I could see the same look of anguish on his face that I saw on Dad's.

We pointed out the doctor's office, but I could tell that Hussein was affected by the meeting. When Hannah, one of his nurses, came by Hussein stopped her.

'Your Highness!' he joked, bowing from the waist. The nurse rolled her eyes and laughed. Hussein had been spending a lot of time with the nursing staff and they were developing a special bond, as well as getting used to his sense of humour.

'Who was that man?'

Hannah explained that he was the father of a girl who was waiting for a valve replacement operation, similar to the one Hussein had received. Hussein looked deep in thought.

'I'm going to talk to him,' he said to me when Hannah had gone. 'I know that look. It's fear. I think I might be able to help.'

And with that Hussein disappeared slowly down the corridor in search of the man.

Worried that he'd overdo it, I had no choice but to follow him. When I caught up, despite only being able to walk very slowly, Hussein was nearly at the doctor's office. The man was there, pacing back and forwards. Just like Dad, I thought.

Hussein went up to the man and gently touched his arm. Embarrassed, I held back and hoped he wouldn't think Hussein was being nosy. What Hannah had said was right: the man's daughter needed a new heart valve and was heading for a big operation. It was the same operation Hussein had had in 2006.

But as Hussein talked to the man, he discovered another coincidence. His daughter had the option of two different valves – the exact choice Hussein had had all those years earlier. I listened as the two got into a long conversation. Hussein told him about his own experience and answered the man's questions from his point of view. Unlike all the doctors and experts this man had listened to, Hussein had been living with one of the valves in his body for several years. He was like a walking review, explaining the differences between the two options and giving the pros and cons. The man was grateful for the information, but he still looked desperately worried. Hussein asked bluntly, 'What is it you're worried about the most?'

The man thought. He seemed to be trying to think of the best way to phrase his answer. Finally he confessed, 'I'm worried that she won't be able to have an ordinary life.'

Hussein looked at him. 'I understand,' he said slowly. 'And she won't.' I was horrified. How could he say this to a man whose daughter was about to have an operation? But I'd forgotten Hussein's sense of humour. Suddenly he smiled. 'She'll have an *extraordinary* life.'

Little did that man know that as he walked down the corridor in the hospital he'd meet someone like Hussein. He was a breath of fresh air – not just because he seemed 'normal' and well, but because he had a gentle sense of humour that made everyone feel at ease. It always amazed me to see first-hand how people reacted to Hussein.

The man asked Hussein if he'd come and meet his daughter and Hussein agreed.

'On one condition,' he said. The man looked puzzled.

'Slow down with your walking! I'm still recovering.'

Hussein went on to spend quite a lot of time with Lizzy, the daughter of the man he met in the corridor, and as time went on we saw the pair come to terms with her operation. Her dad stopped hiding his emotions so much, and their room was filled with laughter as Hussein showed Lizzy that life should never be ordinary.

He told funny stories about doctors getting electric shocks and put them both at their ease. He talked for hours about the differences between the valves and what life was like for him after the operation. The tension we first saw in Lizzy's dad was replaced with laughter, and the gloomy room filled with a sense of hope for life outside the hospital walls.

Lizzy's dad was keen to thank Hussein, but this wasn't part of Hussein's plan. He didn't want any thanks.

'There's nothing to thank me for,' he explained. 'I just want to help another human being who's going through what I am.' He told me afterwards that he got a strange buzz in his heart from helping strangers – I said that must be the pacemaker. He laughed and said it was a good feeling – it was a feeling he wanted to have again. Seeing a positive difference in how Lizzy and her dad felt made him want to do that for others too. The nurses had gone above and beyond to make him better; it was time to pass that kindness on.

For the rest of his stay in Bristol, Hussein had a new purpose. His conversations with the nurses were different and something even changed in the way he carried himself. *'Khastan tavanas tan hast,'* said Mum: 'If you want to chase your dreams you have to believe in them.'

For Hussein a dream did come true out of meeting Lizzy and her dad. After he left Bristol he was put forward for the position of a governor at the hospital, a role that would help to guide the services the hospital provided and represent the community and their views and interests. There would have to be interviews and official documents, but I thought no one could have been more qualified to do the job. At last Hussein felt he was in a position to make a difference.

For Hussein, the most important thing was helping people to feel at home in hospital. He talked a lot about the sense of gloom and doom Lizzy and her dad felt when they arrived, and he knew that was the place to start his new mission. The NHS had given him his life back – twice – but the real gift had been the care and attention of the staff. He said if he could help someone else just a small proportion of the amount he had been helped, then he'd be happy.

Coming back to Cardiff felt unreal. While we'd been away yet again we'd thought we would lose Hussein. Of course, we were grateful that he'd made it, but we were having too many of these close calls.

Hussein, however, barely seemed to notice. He was so energised by the possibility of his new role as a governor that he was like a different person. Dad joked that maybe they'd shocked him a bit too much. He certainly seemed like a man on a mission. But I guessed time was something Hussein never felt like he had much of.

The formalities were completed and University Hospital Bristol finally had a new governor. As Hussein took up his new role, I realised that things hadn't been so bad for us. I'd spent years focusing on what had gone wrong – having to leave Afghanistan so suddenly, being on the road and fighting all the battles that were thrown at us on the way. Then Hussein's illness, the emergencies and long hospital stays. But Hussein made me realise that along the way a lot of people had helped us. People who hadn't asked for anything in return, from our neighbours in Herat to Soran the trafficker to the nurses at Southampton,

Cardiff and Bristol. In many cases we hadn't even been able to thank them.

It's easy to think life's against us when everything's going wrong. But as soon as things go right again, how often do we go straight back to taking life for granted? Seeing Hussein's smile as he left for his first governors' meeting made me realise it doesn't have to be like that. It's just about taking the time to say thank you.

Hussein wasn't like the other governors. He was still a long-term out-patient of the hospital. Sometimes he'd go straight from a cardiology check-up to a governors' meeting, and many of the board members were unaware of this. Just like at school, he hid what was really going on. If he had an attack of arrhythmia or his blood pressure was unstable he'd still walk through those doors wearing his governor's badge. He saw his unique role on the board as being the voice of the patients. He knew what it was like to be in hospital for a long time, and he was focused on making the patient experience a positive one.

Despite the pacemaker working well, Hussein still described his heart as having a mind of its own. Some days it would behave, others it wouldn't. He never knew what sort of day it was going to be when he got up in the morning.

But he saw his role at Bristol as being his destiny. It was what had been missing in his life. Yes, it was a thankless task, but Hussein had no agenda other than wanting to make a positive difference. He couldn't control his heart, but he could control how he lived with it.

Soon, the Heath hospital in Cardiff realised that they also could do with Hussein's knowledge and advice. So the hospital that had cared for him so much in the early days of us arriving in the UK invited Hussein to become a member of their board too.

They soon learnt that it wasn't just knowledge and experience that Hussein could give them. His wit and positivity made board meetings fun, and his compassion for the patients meant he was always invited onto the ward. The doctors and nurses on the cardiology ward – the same place where he'd met the old lady several years ago – loved having him there to speak to patients.

Hussein still had regular 'emergencies', where an arrhythmia attack would get out of control. In these instances Hessam and I knew what to do: keep Mum and Dad calm, call an ambulance and get Hussein to the Heath. The doctors would be ready to shock him if necessary, to reset the rhythm of his heart.

I was rarely very far from Hussein. But in early 2017 I was invited to go snowboarding with some friends in the Alps. It was a long journey, and I hadn't had much sleep. When we got to France at midnight, I was starting to unpack when I had a call from Hessam. He was at home with Hussein.

'What's up?' I asked.

'Hussein's not feeling well,' said Hessam.

I knew what this meant. In our family it was what we said when Hussein had an arrhythmia attack. I panicked. Why wasn't I there? We were supposed to be a team, and now the worst had happened and the team was a man down.

'Ok, okay,' I rushed. 'Have you called the ambulance? Where are Mum and Dad?'

'We're at the hospital now. It wasn't like normal, Hamed. It's worse. It's like it's faster or something. All the colour went from his face.' Here he paused. He could never lie to me. 'They've had to shock him twice.'

I had to get back there. Hussein needed me, and holiday or no holiday I had to be there for him. I'd promised. I managed to find the number for a taxi company and arranged to be picked up and taken to the airport. I had no idea what it would cost. It was snowing hard by now but I knew I had no choice. I told my friends I was leaving and went downstairs to the hotel reception to wait for the taxi.

Everyone told me to wait upstairs and that reception would call me when the taxi got there, but they didn't understand. Even by waiting here I was a step closer to Hussein. A promise is a promise, and by being here, hundreds of miles away when Hussein needed me, I was breaking mine.

By the time the taxi finally arrived the adrenaline was pumping through my body. Lack of sleep and worry about Hussein meant that I was wired with panic. I told the taxi driver to go faster and faster, and the car skidded across the icy roads. I knew it was dangerous, but all I could think of was what if I never saw Hussein again? He'd had episodes like this before, but never when I'd been hundreds of miles away from him.

It took two hours to get to the airport, but it felt like days. The temperature had dropped again as we got into the small hours of the morning, and the driver gripped the wheel as he weaved past other cars. I prayed and prayed, just like I'd done in that prayer room when Hussein had his operation.

When we got to the local airport the car said -12 degrees. There didn't seem to be any lights on anywhere, and the place looked deserted. Finally I saw what looked like a security booth, and I asked the driver to pull up outside it.

'Is this Alpes-Isère airport?' I asked the man in the booth.

He said something in French back to me. I looked pleadingly at the driver. He sighed.

'Yes, he says it is Alpes-Isère airport. But it doesn't open until 7am!'

I started to get my bags together.

'You do know it's only 3am?' asked the driver. 'You've got four hours to wait.'

'I know. I'll wait it out until 7am,' I said. I gave him the cash.

'But it's -12 degrees!' he said. I think he thought I was crazy. But it was a step closer to Hussein – that was all that mattered. As long as I was doing something to get back to him I felt better.

Realising I wasn't going to see sense, the driver at least managed to persuade me to put on some more clothes from my luggage. Wrapped up, I got out of the car and prepared for the wait.

I was glad of the clothes. Before dawn broke it got even colder, and I started to pace backwards and forwards to keep warm. 'I'm just like Dad,' I thought with a grimace.

As 3am became 4am and the night started to fade away, so did I. My pace slowed, I started to feel exhausted, and the cold was creeping into my body like a disease. Without realising it I was putting my own health in a dangerous situation. But all I could think about was Hussein.

At around 4.30am I felt a tap on my shoulder. I was dragging myself past the airport doors for the thousandth time when I turned round and saw the security guard. He'd taken pity on me. In broken English he said, 'You will die here if you do not get warm,' and I realised he was right. He took a bunch of keys and unlocked the main airport door, half pushing me inside. He switched on the heaters and made me sit underneath them. I hadn't realised how dangerously cold I was. I could no longer feel my legs, despite the thermal layers I was wearing. My face was buried into my jacket.

As I started to get warm I began to get the feeling back in my fingers. As I did I felt a vibration in my pocket. My phone! Still shivering, I opened the text from Hessam. It was the news I'd been waiting for.

'Bro is stable.'

I closed my eyes. The relief and the warmth of the room meant that I finally slept, until 7am when the doors were unlocked and people started to arrive at the airport. I made my way to my gate, knowing that in just a few hours I'd be by Hussein's side.

# CHAPTER 25

# Until the end

By the time I reached Cardiff Hussein was out of the woods yet again. But the close calls were getting more frequent – and more serious. As a family we carried on regardless, with an ongoing hope that we could beat this thing, but deep down we were getting more and more worried. And so were the doctors.

When Hussein had his operation in 2006 the doctors had explained to us that it was only a temporary fix. As Hussein continued to grow, his heart would too, and they didn't fully know the effect that would have on his condition. Now, they could see that his heart was having to work too hard. He struggled daily with his breathing, and the constant resets couldn't carry on forever. They were simply running out of options.

Hussein confided in me that he was starting to have dark thoughts. He knew that his heart was warning him that it couldn't cope, and he feared that sooner or later something would give. But he never told anyone else these fears, least of all Mum and Dad. It was the road he was on, and he had to accept it.

Instead, he continued to throw himself into his roles as governor of the two hospitals. While everyone else worried about the future, Hussein's worries were more to do with the present. How would he get to his meetings? Would he manage the stairs? Each time he stayed in hospital he worried that he was missing our night time chats. And of course he worried about Mum and Dad. I could tell the effort it took him to show them he was ok okay, putting on his usual antics throughout the day. I once found him reading papers before a meeting while hooked up to an IV in bed in Cardiff. But still he wouldn't give up. The most important thing for him was to keep giving.

The doctors started talking about another operation. But this time they couldn't just replace valves – it would have to be a transplant. This was a huge decision, and constantly thinking about it put a strain on all of us. We all thought Hussein was crazy when he started planning a holiday to Morocco for the whole family. Wasn't he listening to the doctors? To an outsider it looked like he was pretending nothing was wrong, but I knew the real purpose was to give us all a break. All he wanted was to sit in the sun for a week with his family and put all thoughts of operations out of everyone's mind. He needed a rest from the constant hospital visits and medical discussions. We all did. Was he planning this holiday as one last hurrah? I wondered how many battle scars someone could face before they wave the white flag and say, 'Enough.'

This wasn't the first time we'd talked about a transplant of course. But it felt different this time. It felt like it was the only option left. Hussein was restless. I would sense that he wasn't sleeping, instead spending hours each night lying awake, his mind racing. Sometimes I got up in the night and found him wide awake, his eyes open and searching. I'd try to keep him company then, distracting him and occupying his mind. But I knew Hussein, and I knew that he was thinking about Mum and Dad. As the eldest he always felt he should look after them. I also knew he took our musketeers promise seriously. There was no way he'd want to leave Hessam and me alone.

We were invited to visit a cardiology specialist in Newcastle to discuss transplant options. After examining Hussein and talking to his doctors at Bristol, Southampton and Cardiff, it seemed they thought transplant might be a viable option. We all had many sleepless nights after that. We were told the risks of the operation, but Hessam and I still spent hours googling success rates and complications. The more we knew, the more afraid we were.

For Hussein, it wasn't the idea of the operation itself that was worrying. He told me that the thing he struggled with was the idea of having a new heart. He tapped his chest.

'It's like an old friend, this,' he'd say. 'A bit of a rubbish one, but one that's stuck around. I don't think I want a new one.' I thought about the compassion Hussein had for other people. He needn't worry – you could do a hundred transplants on Hussein, but his true heart would stay the same.

In some ways, all the discussions about a transplant were like background noise to Hussein while he got on with life. His focus was still on his roles as governor, and even if he couldn't make it to the hospital he would call up the nurses. His favourites, Hannah and Beth, loved his jokes. He continued to call them 'Your Highness' and always made them laugh. But behind it all was serious business. Hussein wanted to improve patients' experiences and support the NHS staff he knew worked so hard. Time hadn't stopped for him, so why should it for them? But he couldn't ignore his own health forever. We had to make more and more hospital visits and another trip to Newcastle before the doctors finally agreed that a transplant alone wasn't going to work. Hussein's liver was so damaged that he would also need a liver transplant. Both would have to be done at the same time, an operation rarely done in the UK. No one wanted to ask what the survival rate would be for that, but the procedure was so unusual that I don't think the doctors really knew.

Hussein was spending more and more time in the Heath in Cardiff as his breathing became less stable, and while I badly missed him, there were other problems at home which kept Hessam and me preoccupied. My grandfather in Herat – Mum's dad – had passed away. Mum was grieving, and I knew it wasn't only for him but for everything we'd left behind. It made it even harder for her to deal with Hussein.

I was struggling to sleep at night, and during one restless night while Hussein was staying on the ward my phone rang.

I was awake in seconds, and when I saw that it was a landline my heart sank. That meant the hospital.

I picked up the phone immediately.

'Is that Hamed Amiri?'

I took a long, deep breath in. Something was wrong.

'Yes.'

The voice was gentle. 'We need you to come in please. Your brother isn't feeling well.'

That phrase again. It sounded so innocent, like a child feeling poorly at school. But I knew what it meant.

'Is he ok? Please ... just tell me,' I begged. I couldn't stand another one of these close calls.

'Just come in.'

My heart was racing now. I didn't care about sleep any more, and my mind was all over the place. I needed to calm myself down before waking Mum and Dad.

I managed to put my own emotions aside, as I had done so many times over the years, and gently woke them. Lying to them when I didn't even know the truth myself never got any easier, but I had to tell them everything was okay or Mum would panic.

'It's just another blip,' I said. 'But we need to go in.'

After some discussion we decided that Mum and I would go to the hospital straight away and Dad would get Hessam up and follow after. Dad always struggled to face things head on, and I think he appreciated the delay. I kept telling Mum that Hussein just wasn't feeling well, but she'd been through this so many times alongside me. She knew the score.

It didn't take long to get to the hospital, but all the way I kept telling myself it was just another one of those close calls. We'd been here before; we'd get through it. We just needed to get there.

Making our way straight to the ward that was so familiar, Mum waited by the lift, but I told her I'd take the stairs. I wasn't going to wait for any lift. I ran up two at a time, impatient as ever to be next to my brother. My heart was pounding. What if this time I was too late?

When I saw Hussein he was attached to all sorts of wires. I tried to calm my nerves and sound matter-of-fact.

'Hey, bro, are you okay? What happened?'

'I don't know, I just felt breathless,' he whispered. His hand felt frail in mine.

There was nothing to say so I just sat there, holding his hand.

When Mum arrived I decided to let her sit with him while I went to talk to the doctors. I was proud of her as I watched her hold back her tears and stay positive for Hussein's sake.

Talking to the doctors was usually left to me. Mum and Dad still didn't have brilliant English, and although I'd failed my biology GCSE, I was an expert in the terms of Hussein's condition. Ever since his operation in 2006 I'd listened to every word, researched every issue and made sure that I understood what they were talking about. I'd picked up a lot, and I knew how to work out how bad it was.

I went to the nurses' station first.

'What's happened? Please tell me the truth,' I whispered to the nurse on duty. I hoped she'd follow suit and keep her voice down. I didn't want Mum hearing anything.

Thankfully, the nurse spoke quietly. But as much as she

wanted to tell me what was going on and put my mind at rest, she had no idea what had caused this latest episode. We just had to wait for the doctors to come and assess Hussein. It was the middle of the night, so the doctor on call had to be contacted. I was frustrated. I had so many questions. Did Hussein need to have the medication filtered from his bloodstream again? Or were we at the point where he needed an urgent transplant? The nurse smiled, compassion visible in her eyes. She just said we had to wait and see.

The next hour was agony. I let Dad and Hessam know that Hussein was 'okay' and settled down for another wait. I didn't even know what 'okay' meant.

Mum was just about holding it together. But I could tell that, while she was telling herself that everything would be fine, deep down she was in pieces. Hussein was still her little boy.

Knowing his condition was critical, the nurses decided to move Hussein into the CCU while we waited for the doctors on call to assess him. I knew what CCU meant – it meant they thought he could crash at any moment. I called Hessam to update him.

Then suddenly everything became urgent. The nurses were rushing Hussein through the sealed doors and they told Mum to stay behind. Heartbroken at having to leave her son, Mum finally let her calm façade drop. I frantically called Hessam again.

Thankfully, as I dialled Hessam arrived with Dad. They'd missed Hussein going into the CCU by seconds. Once again, the four of us were left outside those double doors, wondering what was happening on the other side.

I tried to stay positive for Mum and Dad's sake, but I couldn't shake the feeling that this time was different. I knew how precarious Hussein's condition was at the moment, and how weak his heart had become. I also knew his liver was in a dangerously poor condition. But my focus had to be keeping Mum and Dad calm. Mum prayed silently, her lips moving, while Dad took up his usual pacing. In my head I was going through every possible outcome and how I would deal with it, trying to think how I could best protect Mum and Dad. I remembered Hussein telling me how much they'd sacrificed to get us here, and how it was my job to shield them from whatever lay ahead.

I thought about how close we were as a family, and how everything we'd been through had made us stronger. Unlike most Afghan families, we no longer had aunties and uncles and cousins to support us. Ever since we'd arrived in the UK it had just been us. What I would give now for an annoying cousin or an interfering aunty to lean on! I felt like I couldn't support Mum by myself. I started to wonder how she would cope if that turned out to be the last time she saw her son. Why couldn't we just have some news?

I pressed the buzzer at the double doors impatiently. To my surprise, after two or three rings someone answered. I rested my head against the intercom.

'Please, can someone tell us what's going on?' I tried desperately not to cry.

Suddenly the door opened. It was one of the nurses, but all she could say was, 'We still don't know. I'm so sorry. We've paged Dr Masani and he's on his way.' She paused. 'Hussein's still not stable but he is okay,' she added. Then she went back in.

I longed to follow her back to the CCU. I just wanted to see Hussein for myself. Knowing Mum and Dad were waiting for news, I composed my face and turned to talk to them.

'They're still setting up the machines and running some tests,' I said. 'He's stable.' Hessam's look told me that he knew I was lying, but we both knew it was necessary. Over the years we'd developed a sort of language of our own when it came to Hussein. 'Stable' could mean anything.

Dad set off on his pacing again and Mum knelt and prayed, hoping her voice would be heard as it had been so many times before. With both of them distracted, I called Hessam over.

Hessam had always been my little brother. Through all our travels to get to the UK we'd treated him as the baby. But here he was, nearly a man. I wanted to confide in him as an equal, but as ever I was torn between protecting my little brother and wanting to share the burden of my emotions. I decided that Hessam was old enough to be treated like an adult. Besides, I needed an ally.

'Don't say anything to Mum and Dad, please, but I have a bad feeling about this,' I whispered. Hessam looked me in the eyes. Even saying that made me feel like I was betraying Hussein, as if I was somehow admitting that he wasn't strong enough to fight any more. Hessam nodded. I wondered whether he felt it too.

'Whatever happens, we've got to be there for Mum and Dad,' I continued. 'We can worry about ourselves later.' I realised that's exactly what Hussein would have said to me.

I felt guilty for telling Hessam about negative thoughts. Not only was I not there to protect my big brother when he needed me, but I'd let my little brother down, too. I tried to push it out of my mind. The priority now was looking after Mum and Dad like Hussein wanted.

I could tell Mum was struggling. She'd only just lost her own father, and this added stress was too much. I wished again that we had some family close by to help. We don't tend to realise the value of family until we haven't got it any more.

That was it! I suddenly realised what would help Mum. If I could somehow get her to hear a familiar voice it might help her to stay calm. I thought of her sister, my *khale*, who had moved to live in Iran. If I could get hold of her on the phone it would mean the world to Mum.

I got my phone and tried to work out the time difference. I couldn't, but I dialled my aunt anyway. She wouldn't be expecting a call from her sister, especially if it was the middle of the night, but I hoped she'd pick up anyway. Sure enough, after a few rings, a sleepy voice answered the phone. I immediately passed the phone to Mum, and as soon as she heard her sister's voice she broke down in tears. Not being with her father when he passed away had been very hard for her and she'd missed being able to grieve with her siblings.

Mum and *khale* spoke for a few minutes in Farsi, but I could tell that *khale* was asking about Hussein. Mum couldn't say much as every time she tried to talk about it she became too emotional. Eventually I took the phone.

'*Khale*, how are you?' I said brightly. I don't know why I was trying to sound so casual – she must have known something was terribly wrong.

'What has happened, Hamed? Please tell me.' I knew she could sense the tremor in my voice.

I locked my jaw and tried not to cry. 'It's Hussein,' I said hoarsely. 'He's not well.'

Just like us, she understood what this meant. She started to cry quietly, and I wondered whether I'd done the right thing in ringing her. I explained what was going on and that the doctors weren't sure what to do. He was really sick this time.

*Khale* seemed to sense my foreboding. 'Please tell me he's ok, Hamed. Can I at least talk to him one last time?' *One last time?* I couldn't control my emotions any longer. Hearing her say that was like a knife in my chest. Tears started to stream down my face. I tried to explain what had happened and why we couldn't get to Hussein at the moment. But still she begged to hear Hussein's voice.

'*Khale*, I will try,' I told her. 'But please don't say "one last time".' My voice was shaking. 'He'll be okay, *Inshallah*, he has to be. Just speak to Mum for a minute.'

I handed the phone back to Mum and rushed out of the corridor. What if I'd spoken to Hussein for the last time too? I couldn't bear the thought of no more night time chats with my brother, no more laughter, no more jokes. I couldn't imagine not seeing his cheeky smile again.

I tried to compose myself enough to go back to Mum. There were no nurses in sight, just a long, lonely corridor, and I wished Hussein was there to lighten the mood as he always did. I didn't know what to do. The only thing I could think of was praying to God that he'd pull through once again. Despite everything, I still believed there was a God, and that he was up there looking after my brother. I still believed he had a plan for everything. I just wished there were more people to pray – more voices to speak up for Hussein.

Then I did something I'd never done before. I reached for my phone and logged on to Facebook. I'd always been very private on social media, never sharing anything about how I really felt. But this was different. We needed as many people behind Hussein as possible. So I wrote a post, asking – begging – anyone who was awake to pray for my big brother.

This last plea done, I put my phone away and went back to Mum and Dad. I'd been away too long – maybe there was news.

I can only think that God must have been listening, because as I turned towards the double doors they opened, and Dr Masani came out. I almost hugged him. If anyone could find out what was wrong with Hussein it was him.

Dr Masani took us into the waiting room and we all sat down. I felt sick in my stomach.

'Can I just close the door?' he said quietly. He seemed to be gathering his thoughts.

The four of us just sat in silence, willing him to say something. I couldn't bear it.

'Doctor, just tell us what's happened. Do you know yet?' I asked.

Dr Masani paused. Then he explained, 'Hussein's sudden deterioration is because he's struggling for oxygen. His heart is no longer responding to the pacemaker and it's having to work so hard that it's not able to get enough oxygen around his body. We're having to give him adrenaline just to keep it going.'

I didn't understand. After everything I'd learnt and understood about Hussein's condition, somehow this was too complicated. I only wanted to know one thing.

'But is he going to be ok? Is the pacemaker failing?'

By now, Dr Masani had known our family for almost fifteen years. He'd been through all the close calls, all the emergencies, all the blue lights. He knew when he had to be honest. He looked at me, then turned to Mum and Dad.

'Hussein's pacemaker is working fine. But I think his heart has had enough.'

I stared at him. Then I looked at Dad, remembering that I had to translate so he could understand. But from the look on Dad's face I didn't need to. They both understood.

I stared back at Dr Masani. Beside me, I was aware that the others were doing the same. For a minute we were all silent. Was this it? The end of the road? Surely not. Surely there was something else they could do? I felt the sickness right inside my core. Then my mind took over, trying to find the logic in what Dr Masani had just said. Maybe he meant that Hussein would have to have a transplant and it would all be okay? Maybe this was just the next phase?

I knew that I was wrong. If we agreed to a transplant it could take months for a heart to become available. And his liver needed to be replaced too. There wasn't time. I tried to stay calm, but inside I wanted to scream.

Whether to break the silence or because he felt we needed to know, Dr Masani started going through the details of what was happening in Hussein's body. Somehow, we all held it together enough to nod along. It was like each of us was trying to be strong for the others. I could hear what Dr Masani was saying, but I knew that we were all just pretending to listen. It was like there were bubbles inside my chest and any minute they would burst and come out. I had to hold them in.

Suddenly I couldn't take it any more. I interrupted him with my usual question. 'So, what's next?'

Dr Masani paused again. It seemed like ages.

'All we can do is monitor. For the next few hours at least we just need to see if the adrenaline can make Hussein's heart respond to the pacemaker again.'

So that was it again. It all boiled down to hope. It was all we had. No fancy medical terms, no theories, just blind hope. I suddenly sensed that Dad was panicking. He wanted to get out of that room. I tried to wrap things up.

'Do you have any more questions?' Dr Masani asked gently. I shook my head. As soon as I did so, Dad more or less bolted from the room. I quickly told Hessam to go after him so I could stay with Mum. We had to somehow hold it together for them.

Dr Masani told us that we probably needed some space as a family, but that after that we could go in to see Hussein. Finally, I thought. Mum would get to see her boy and I could be by his side once again. I went to find Dad and Hessam.

Thankfully they hadn't gone far, and I brought them back into the waiting room to be with Mum. As we waited to go in and see Hussein we gathered in a circle, just like we always used to do around the *sofra*. There in the quietness we looked into one another's eyes. We'd get through this, I thought. We had to. I knew I'd do anything to fill that void in the circle where Hussein was supposed to be.

Then Dad said something I never thought I'd hear him say. Something that made me realise he was finally learning to face things head on.

'Hamed, please will you let people know that Hussein might only have a few hours?'

Tears were pouring down his face, and it was all I could do to stop myself from crying. Was that it? A few hours? I couldn't accept that this was the end, that there was nothing more they could do. But I knew that Dad had given me a job to do, and like always I didn't want to let him down. I silently took my phone and left the room.

Once out in the corridor, I suddenly realised that I didn't know who to call. I walked around the corridor, trying to think what to do. I just wanted to be in there with Hussein, but I knew that Dad felt this was important.

What would I even say? How could I tell our relatives that their nephew and cousin might have only a few hours left to live? How would I even say it? 'My big brother only has a few hours'? Those words didn't sound right. They couldn't be true. I wasn't sure I could do it.

I decided to call *khale* first. My fingers numb, I found the number on my phone and redialled, knowing there'd be no delay in her answering this time. Sure enough, she picked up immediately.

'Fariba?'

'No, *khale*, it's Hamed.'

'What's happened?' She sounded broken and tearful.

'*Khale*, it's not good. They have said he only has a few hours.' I couldn't believe these words were actually coming out of my mouth. I held my breath to stop myself from crying.

All I could hear on the other end was *khale* sobbing. Between the tears I could just make out her begging me to let her hear Hussein's voice once more. But I knew this wasn't possible.

'He's too sick, *khale*,' I said.

Then I told her I had to go, and like a robot I moved on to the next call. Time was ticking on, and I didn't want to miss my chance to see Hussein. I made call after call, first to my uncles, then to various cousins.

And so I progressed through all our extended family in Afghanistan, Iran and other countries, calmly telling them that my amazing big brother was about to die. It was the hardest thing I'd ever done. Everyone in our family loved Hussein. How could they not? He was the funniest, the smartest, the most alive. He was the kindest person any of us had ever known. The thought of him leaving us was unbearable. And yet somewhere, deep inside my shattered heart, I found something that made me carry on. I think it was the thought that, if I didn't do this, Mum or Dad would have to. And Hessam and I had agreed that we'd put them first.

My calls done, I slowly made my way back to the waiting room to find Mum and Dad. Wiping my eyes as I went, I suddenly saw a nurse coming out of the doors of the CCU. Not wanting to wait any longer, I stopped her.

'Please. Can we go and see Hussein now?' I pointed to Mum, whose praying figure was just visible through the waiting room door.

'Yes, two at a time,' she nodded. She smiled at me so sadly. I rushed through to Mum.

'We can go and see him,' I said. She stood up quickly, wiping her tears. I knew she wouldn't want Hussein to see her so upset. As we walked through the corridor neither of us knew what to expect. How would Hussein look? He'd never been this sick before, and I worried that he would just be a mass of wires and tubes.

Dad stayed behind with Hessam, terrified as usual of seeing his son in pain. I was secretly glad, as I couldn't stand the ache of not being near Hussein for much longer.

Guided by the nurses, Mum and I made our way into the CCU room. Mum instinctively turned right as soon as we got in there, and I realised that only a mother would know exactly where her child would be.

And there he was, her baby, half-awake, with tubes coming out of him, while the nurses and doctors watched over him like guardians.

Without saying a word Mum went over to Hussein and took him in her arms. I heard her whisper ever so quietly, 'It's okay, Mummy's here.'

Then Hussein whispered back, so quietly and hoarsely that I could hardly hear him. 'Hey Mum, where you been?' Even with all the tubes coming out of him he managed a smile.

'I'm right here, baby,' Mum said. Tears were running down her face.

Then Hussein saw me. 'Hey bro, you good?' I said. He took my hand. I had to hold back my tears, but I also knew that even on strong medication Hussein would know how I was feeling.

'Yeah, I'm fine, bro. We've been here before!' Hussein smiled calmly, still clutching onto my hand.

For a moment then, all the noise and people seemed to disappear and we were overtaken by a moment of calm.

The nurses seemed to sense the gap in the circle, and within minutes they'd gone out to fetch Dad and Hessam. Suddenly all five of us were together, forming our familiar family circle.

Instead of looking at each other, we all just held on to Hussein, gazing at him with unconditional love. 'We're all here, bro, by your side, no matter how tough it gets,' Hessam whispered, and I remembered that moment when we'd promised to be musketeers.

Then we fell silent, and we all held on to each other, each one gripping an arm or a hand. Tears were streaming down the faces of the nurses, who watched from a short, careful distance.

Then it was time for the circle to break. The nurses gently asked if they could run a couple of tests on Hussein, and we all moved out of the way. Dad could no longer keep his emotions at bay, and he took that moment to go out and compose himself.

While the nurses were checking some monitors, Hussein said to Mum, 'Can I just talk to my brothers for a minute?'

Mum smiled. She knew the special bond between us. 'I'm just outside,' she said, and kissed Hussein on the forehead before reluctantly walking away.

'Come closer,' Hussein said to Hessam, and we both took hold of his hands. I tried to forget what the doctor had said and pretend that this was just another brotherly pep talk.

'I'm going to talk, okay? So I just want you to listen – and don't argue back,' Hussein said. He smiled weakly.

Hessam and I nodded gently.

'I want you to forgive me for whatever I've done in the past that might have hurt you. And I want you to look after Mum and Dad after I'm gone ...'

I had to interrupt. 'Bro, please don't talk like that ...' Tears were flowing uncontrollably down my face. Hussein looked impatient.

'Just shut up and listen for once!' he smiled.

'Get married. Bring some happiness to them, please, and if I've upset anyone please ask them for my forgiveness. Oh, and look after Moe ... he will find it tough being on his own!' He was so calm as always. Hessam and I were weeping uncontrollably. This couldn't be it. This couldn't be goodbye.

Although I'd always had to look after Hussein because of his illness, it had always been him who'd watched over me. Hot-headed and impatient, I needed Hussein to calm me down and talk sense into me. He was the only one who knew how to do it. Despite his heart, I'd always seen him as the stronger one. He always pulled through, always made the most of things, always put others first. He wasn't just my brother, my role model, my roommate. He was my hero.

Standing there, hearing him speak those terrible words, I just wanted the ground to open up and eat me. I didn't want to go on without Hussein. What would be the point?

Not wanting to upset him, I held on to his hand and nodded. He knew me. He'd know what I was thinking.

Suddenly a doctor came in, and the spell that had kept Hessam and me glued to Hussein's side was broken. But I had one more thing to say to Hussein before Mum and Dad came back in. I moved over so the doctor could do his checks.

'You know I love you, bro? And I'm here, no matter what, till the end.' Hussein just smiled. He'd taught me that.

The three of us had one more hug before Hussein said, 'We'd better get Mum back in, she'll be going mental.' We all laughed through our tears. I knew I'd remember those smiles forever.

Hessam went to get Mum and Dad and brought them back in. I used those few moments to try and regain my composure. As Mum came back in, Hussein turned his attention once again to her.

'Hey Mum, everything will be ok, you know,' he smiled. Mum couldn't speak, but just bent down and kissed Hussein on his forehead. As she did, Hussein looked over her shoulder at me. For a minute his eyes locked with mine, and I knew that he knew something was about to happen. We'd always been able to communicate like that, without a word.

I noticed that as he hugged her Hussein was clutching Mum harder and harder. Then suddenly some beeps went off. The doctors calmly came over.

I reached for Mum and pulled her away then. She didn't want to go, but I knew Hussein needed the doctors. I turned her away, blocking her eyes with a hug as the doctors did everything they could. And I knew I'd kept my promise. I'd stayed by my brother's side until the end.

# EPILOGUE

In the weeks that followed, our time was taken up looking after Mum and Dad. We'd promised Hussein we'd care for them, and Hessam and I had also agreed that we'd deal with our own feelings later.

There was a lot to do. But I was grieving for my brother in a way I'd never thought possible. We'd promised Hussein that we'd stick together until the end, and we had. But apart from that last conversation, we'd never discussed what we were supposed to do after the end. The one person who'd know what to do was the one person who wasn't there.

Those days felt empty. I missed being able to chat with Hussein about anything, and life without him felt flat and pointless. He was the only one who could have made it better, but he was the one I couldn't turn to.

But as time went on things started to happen. We discovered other areas of Hussein's life we hadn't even known about. Strangers poured out their grief online and in person. We learnt how Hussein had brightened the day of the waitresses who worked in the local café, and how he'd always paid for a fellow student's lunch when he'd hit hard times. We heard from the lady on the market stall who told us how Hussein had helped her daughter, and from countless patients and hospital staff who Hussein had supported.

Hannah and Beth, the nurses who loved Hussein and cared for him in so many ways, ran a half marathon in his memory, raising over £3,000 for the NHS.

During those weeks we found out more about our brother than we'd known when he was alive. We discovered that his heart had reached further and wider than anyone could have known. Although his real heart had failed, this other heart – the one that cared unconditionally for the people around him – was still here.

It was time for a new pact. From that day, Hessam and I made a promise to ensure our brother wasn't forgotten. We would do everything we could to create a legacy for Hussein's life and ensure that his second heart would live on.

For Hessam, that meant continuing Hussein's work with the hospitals he was involved with. He took steps to become a governor for NHS Bristol, the very role that Hussein had done with such compassion. His first board meeting, sitting in the very seat where Hussein had sat so many times, was a momentous occasion.

As for me, my goal was to celebrate Hussein and share his story with as many people as possible. We knew that Hussein's passion was always to help others. So that's what we'd do. But we'd also make sure that Mum and Dad remembered his life as filled with laughter and love rather than sadness and sorrow.

I decided to write. I would share the story of our family's journey to the UK and Hussein's own personal journey trying to overcome his illness. I'd write about the lessons Hussein taught me, and the positivity he brought to life. Getting my thoughts on paper helped me to process everything that had happened, but over time I realised that other people should hear about this boy with two hearts too.

BBC coverage of the nurses' half marathon led to more publicity about Hussein. This led to a production company creating a documentary film which will be commissioned by the BBC and shortly afterwards the Wales Millennium Centre, one of the biggest theatre venues in Europe, creating a stage adaptation of Hussein's story. Finally, a meeting with developmental editor Sophie Bradshaw and publisher Icon Books led to the book being published.

Hussein's story isn't just about our family. It isn't even about the incredible love that underpinned everything as we fought for our freedom. It's about a journey into hope, and a love for life even when life is hard.

Love is a strange thing, especially when it's felt between total strangers. In my life with Hussein and through writing this book, I can see now that love crosses borders. It crosses religions and families, and can occur between people who'll never see each other again. It brings hope, even in the darkest moments you can face.

Love is also contagious, jumping from one person to the next and never dying out. Hussein spread love to many people in his life. I caught it too, and through his story I hope it can be passed on forever.

# ACKNOWLEDGEMENTS

First and foremost, praises and thanks to God, the Almighty, for giving me the strength that I so badly needed during the darkest moments in my life.

Mum and Dad – you have done so much for all three of us over the years, from making sacrifices beyond my comprehension to always being there to protect us. Hussein, you will never read this but I know you are somewhere up there looking after us. While you were here you were always there for me, even though at times I didn't see it and after you left us you somehow not only gave me the strength to get through your loss but the drive to make sure your legacy lives on. Sharing your wisdom, laughter, unconditional love and strong will is the true purpose of this book. Hessam, my younger brother, you have stood by me like a rock. The countless hours we have spent re-living those dark moments have been some of the hardest we have had to endure but I know I only managed it with you being there.

Danial Khoshkhou, Fahim, I know Hussein was like a brother to you both and I can't thank you enough for believing in this book, fuelling my fire and offering advice in my low moments.

Azzy, your friendship, advice and constant presence over the years has helped me more than you can ever imagine. Yours has been the voice on the phone whenever I needed it.

Mo Jannah, we are only getting started on our journey but already your crazy vision and belief has helped me see this through.

Samantha Toombs – thank you! I know you think you didn't do anything but making me look forward and always pushing me to put my thoughts into words eventually resulted in this book and that wouldn't have happened without you.

Amy Salter, somehow in a very short period of time you not only became my go-to person for advice, but also the voice I would always seek out for encouragement.

Sophie Bradshaw, I don't even know how to thank you. Not only did you believe in my story but you brought it to life, taking my chaotic, emotional words and turning them into a beautiful piece of writing.

This acknowledgment wouldn't be complete without mentioning Ellen Conlon and Icon Books. Thank you for taking on my story and helping to share it with the rest of the world.

# ABOUT THE AUTHOR

**Hamed Amiri** was born in Herat, Afghanistan, in late 1989 and grew up under Taliban rule before fleeing to the UK at the age of ten. Despite his traumatic childhood and disruptions to his education, in 2011 he gained a BA in Computer Science from the University of Glamorgan and now works as a Senior IT manager at NewLaw.

Hamed has become a role model for the younger generation and an influencer in the education sector. He is a board member at Coleg Gwent and a motivational speaker in schools and universities. In 2016 he was awarded the Inspiring the Next Generation Award by the University of South Wales for services to education and young people. Inspired by his late brother's passion for positive change in society, Hamed's mission is to share his family's story with a wider audience and change perceptions surrounding refugees and diversity. This is his first book.